PEAK ENCOUNTERS:

A Spiritual Field Guide for Adventurous Souls

*31 Inspirational Reflections
to Connect You with
God through the Beauty of Nature*

Heather J. Makowicz

XULON PRESS

DEDICATION

∽∞∾

I dedicate this book first, to my Lord and Savior, Jesus Christ, to whom all peak encounters flow.

Secondly, to my family David, Nathaniel, Noah, and Hope Therese, who inspire me every day to be the woman and mother God has called me. May you always be aware of those gentle touchpoints that God provides through the gift of beauty in all of Creation.

Xulon Press
2301 Lucien Way #415
Maitland, FL 32751
407.339.4217
www.xulonpress.com

Printed in the United States of America

Paperback ISBN-13: 978-1-6628-1439-6
Ebook ISBN-13: 978-1-6628-1440-2

TABLE OF CONTENTS

Introduction xi
Entry #1   A Pilgrim's Journey – John Chesters 1
Entry #2   Care of Creation – Ricardo Simmonds 6
Entry # 3   Appalachian Mountain Road – Jeff Klein 11
Entry # 4   Rustic Cabin – Jen Messing........................ 16
Entry #5   Dark Stroll – Sean Cavanaugh 21
Entry #6   Walk through the Seasons –Bill Donaghy.......... 27
Entry #7   Bus to Umbria – Kelly Wahlquist 35
Entry #8   Scuba Diving – Elizabeth Hoisington 40
Entry #9   Star Gazing – Mickey Fairorth 45
Entry #10   Hot Air Balloon – Heather Makowicz.............. 51
Entry #11   Backpacking – Trix 55
Entry #12   Canyoneering – Heather Makowicz 61
Entry #13   Rock Climbing – Chiara Cardone 65
Entry #14   Mountain Climbing – James Delaney............. 72
Entry #15   Whitewater Rafting–Christin Zimmer 78
Entry # 16 Surfing –Bear Woznick........................... 83
Entry # 17 Sailing – Sarah Christmyer 96
Entry #18   Caving – Tom Zimmer...........................100
Entry #19   Ice Climbing –Fr. Nathan Cromly................106
Entry #20   Desert Trek – Heather Makowicz 113
Entry #21   Paddle Boarding –Heather Makowicz 117
Entry #22   Stemming – Heather Makowicz.................122
Entry #23   Fishing – Lori Blake Tedjeske 128
Entry #24   Photography – Brett Illig........................133
Entry #25   Watching Birds – Fr. Henry M. Jordanek..........138

Entry #26   Sunset – Jeannine Peters...........................145
Entry #27   Waterfall Plunge – Heather Makowicz............150
Entry #28   Zip Lining – Heather Makowicz..................155
Entry #29   The Bench –Elizabeth Hoisington 160
Entry #30   Sunrise – Megan Schreiber 166
Entry #31   Gardening – Chiara Cardone.....................170
Contributor's Listed in Order of Entries 176
Works Cited..179

"But ask the animals, and they will teach you, or the birds in the sky and they will tell you, or speak to the earth, and it will teach you or let the fish in the sea inform you. Which of all these does not know the hand of the Lord has done this? In his hand is the life of every creature and breath of all mankind." Job 12:7-10

∞

Saint John Paul II states, "The aesthetic value of creation cannot be overlooked. Our very contact with nature has a deep restorative power; contemplation of its magnificence imparts peace and serenity. The Bible speaks again and again of the goodness and beauty of creation, which is called to glorify God." (*World Day of Peace* 14).

INTRODUCTION

∞

W elcome! Before you begin, consider with an open mind how ready you are for a rich encounter with the living God. Our Creator is endlessly inviting us to be in a relationship with himself. Consider this as an invitation to a "peak experience," a point of meaningful connection with Him.

Nature is one of many ways we can connect with God's still, small voice. Don't worry about trying to define your relationship with God at this point. Let this encounter develop naturally, knowing that God is always ready to meet you where you are.

Maybe you are on the fence about whether God actually exists, if he is relevant today, or just an antiquated idea. Perhaps you have been curious about who God is, but just aren't sure how nature can be connected somehow. Sometimes, you might just "see" or "sense" communion with God, but you don't know how to explain it to others. Allow yourself to be curious, to notice what's coming up, and to give yourself space to be real with whatever desire is stirring within you. This yearning was created in you on purpose. I encourage you to stay close to this desire, it is a beckoning of the One who created us, a God who wants to fill that desire to make us whole.

In developing this book, I invited some friends and ministry partners to join me in sharing how they have been touched, supported, and even transformed in some way by their experiences in the beauty of God's incredible creation. Through His creative, efficacious love, God provides access points to connect with each of us according to our need, whether it is through His Word, and the Sacraments, or through the beauty of the arts, music, and in this case, nature.

SUGGESTIONS BEFORE BEGINNING...

1) Create Space
   A physical space that is comfortable, relaxing, and aesthetically pleasing
   (Ex: a couch with a candle – setting aside this space as sacred to connect with God)

2) Breathe and Invite
   -Become aware of any tension you may be holding in your body. Breathe in as you invite God to be with you on this day. Then, breathe out any anxieties, worries, and preoccupations you may be having and place them in the care of God for now.

3) Commit to a Daily Time
   - Pick a time in the day that you are you are most awake, alert, and least distracted
   -silence can be very helpful to hear the small, subtle voice of God

4) Intention
   - Consider why you may be taking this 31-day journey and what you hope you will gain when you complete it. When we set an intention for the things that we do, it gives us meaning and purpose. We begin to seek the answers we are hoping to find and realize when we look back, the great deal of progress that we've made.

5) Openness and Flexibility
   -Whether you are skeptical, on the fence, or all in with God, allow yourself the opportunity to shift perspectives, and to learn something new. Honesty and authenticity count! Engage with God right where you are, you might be surprised what he has in store for you personally!

6) Ask God to help you with all the above steps. He is waiting.

7) Embark and Exit – hasta la vista baby!

May God's peace be with you and let the adventure begin!
Heather

To learn more about Heather Makowicz
Website: www.heathermakowicz.com
To learn more about Peak Encounter Ministries
Website: www.peakencounter.org
Email: hello@peakencounter.org

*Note: Each entry is presented in the voice of the author so you can better experience their adventure.

A PILGRIM'S JOURNEY*

∞

"Call to me and I will answer you, and will tell you
great and hidden things which you have not known."
Jeremiah 3:33 (ESV)

I n May of 2019, I made my way alone to the seaside town of Baiona,
Spain with just enough belongings to fit in my carry-on sized backpack. Baiona marks the start of the last 80 miles (128 km) to Santiago
de Compostela along the Portuguese Coastal Camino. As I readied
myself that night to begin walking the next morning, I still wasn't sure
what I desired to receive from this Camino experience. I just knew that

for the past seven months, I felt the need to walk solo on the Costal Camino, one of the least popular routes.

The first few days of walking were certainly scarce of pilgrims, and with the ocean on the left to guide me, I could let my mind wander freely. These days featured significant stretches of walking on board-walks and concrete promenades along the beach. The weather was ideal with vibrant blue skies and temperatures in the high 70's. The winds blowing inland from the water were strong enough that I had to frequently tighten the chinstrap on my wide brimmed hat. As I looked out at the Atlantic Ocean, I thought about the vastness of the space between myself and the life I had intentionally paused with on the other side. The gentle sounds of the waves, the emptiness on the horizon, the clarity of the sky, the stiff breeze, and the solitude of the walk were perfect ingredients in a recipe for letting go. I found myself decluttering the busyness of life, making room to receive the presence of God. He was beckoning me to hear Him in words I have heard from Psalm 46:10, to "Be still, and know that I am God"

The tone of the second half of the walk moved from stillness to listening to my fellow travelers and their stories. Through their witness, I expanded my perspective about life, affording me to opportunity to explore areas I had yet to tap into. I was reminded of the prophet Jeremiah heard God say, "Call to me and I will answer you, and will tell you great and hidden things which you have not known." Jeremiah 3:33 (ESV)

One of the days I met Jeff. He was an Englishman in his mid-50's. He was going through a both a divorce and a career transition. We had a long chat and at one point, he asked about the stamps he needed to get the Compostela. After realizing he didn't have enough stamps, looking through his aviator sunglasses, he said to me "It's really not about the certificate, is it?" In that revelation, there was a deep knowing, it seems that each pilgrim comes to understand. The journey is less about what you accomplish, and more about getting in touch with how you are being transformed within. From that moment, we continued to take the last leg of the journey to the Santiago de Compostela, where the famous cathedral of St. James was located.

When we arrived, we had our pictures taken in front of the cathedral of St. James. Typically, it is customary to attend a large Pilgrim

Mass, however, the interior of the cathedral was being renovated that year. Instead, I found a small, windowless chapel where I attended Mass and prayed during my time in the city. This chapel was the place of worship for about twenty semi-cloistered Benedictine Sisters. Instead of the customary 1,200 pilgrims in the big cathedral, this chapel hosted only twenty pilgrims. It was here that I met John, a stoutly built Australian in his late 60s. One of the pilgrims I had a chance to talk with at length after Masses was John, an Australian in his late 60's.

In our conversations, John was very open about his struggles in life and how his persistent faith led him to be grateful for the ability to forgive those who had harmed him in many ways, creating the space to move forward in life. He recalled a leg of his journey where he met Thomas, a German man in his mid-20s. Thomas ventured on the El Camino, seeking direction for his life. As Thomas and John approached the city, Thomas began to sob. When John asked him why he was crying, Thomas exclaimed, "I reached the end and I still don't know what I'm supposed to do with my life." John resolutely yelled, "Thomas! You have to make a decision, or you are going to be walking your entire life!" Wow, what a statement and a conviction to remember!

John then turned to me, he asked me how I would live life differently now that I had this experience. Reflecting on that question, I recalled times I have traveled places before, where the quest was the destination. In contrast, at the end of a pilgrimage, you prepare for a new beginning. Jeff was right! The Camino wasn't about the Compostela, the stamps, or the fanfare of the Pilgrim Mass. My Camino was about learning to make the decision to practice being still and listening to God. We don't need to have all the answers right now or figure everything out on our own. We can find our purpose by deciding to practice letting Christ into our lives.

REFLECTION

PAUSE:

Spend a few minutes in silence, settling into a comfortable place where you can allow your body to relax. If there are a few areas that you are still tight or tense, notice that and take a couple deep breaths to release the tension and offer it to God.

PONDER:

- After reading the story, what struck you the most?
- Were there some themes you resonated with?
- Themes that you noticed a resistance within you?
- I invite you to read Philippians 4:6-7

Do not be anxious about anything, but in everything by prayer and supplication with thanksgiving let your requests be made known to God. And the peace of God, which surpasses all understanding, will guard your hearts and your minds in Christ Jesus."

What word or phrase stood out for you?

PRAY:

Talk with God about it; then, ask God what he would like to say to you about it?

PRACTICE:

Together with God, consider one concrete action step you can take today based on what you heard, read, or experienced during this time.

CLOSING PRAYER (OPTIONAL OR YOUR OWN):

Lord, thank you for being with me in the storms of life! Help me to keep my eyes on you at all times. I want to set my course by your guidance and not in reaction to the disturbance around me. Right now, I'm feeling [tell him your situation]. Please give me your "peace that passes understanding" along with the grace I need to ride the waves to you. In Jesus' name, Amen!

John Chesters: Camino de Santiago, Spain

JOURNAL ENTRY

Entry # 2

CARE OF CREATION*

∞

"In the hand is the life of every creature
and the breath of all mankind."
Job 12: 9-10 (NIV)

When Pope Francis was a young priest in Argentina, he was appointed rector of the Jesuit seminary. One of the first things he did was to convert the seminary grounds into a farm where "students collected honey, milked cows, and cleaned out the pigsty [and] where they often met the rector in his plastic boots" (Ivereigh 178). For young Fr. Bergoglio caring for the farm meant learning humility, being in touch with the poor, feeding the hungry, and finding an ideal space for prayer and contemplation – a place where the word of the Gospel became flesh. One could make the case that the Pope's encyclical

Laudato Si' and integral ecology were already taking shape in his farm experiment. The experiment worked, the seminary boomed, and there was a huge increase in vocations.

The idea that Christian prayer must be connected to the created world is also central to Pope Francis' message for the "World Day of Prayer for the Care of Creation," whose one-year anniversary we celebrated in September, 2016. Quoting *Laudato Si'* the Pope reminded us that "the life of the spirit is not dissociated from the body or from nature" and that Christians are called to a profound "spiritual conversion... whereby the effects of their encounter with Jesus Christ become evident in their relationship with the world around them." Doesn't this sound like something the Pope could be teaching the seminarians at the farm?

More important than the farm itself is the ideal behind it, which has to do with the relationship between prayer and creation. I will call this ideal "prayer in the flesh," taken from the title of a talk by Fr. Bergoglio. His point was that some Christians are unaware that they suffer from a modern heresy he calls 'neodocetism' and that we need to bring prayer to the level of concreteness, to the level of our bodies. We can pray when we touch the hands of a beggar, walk on trails, clean a pigsty, eat with the hungry, milk a cow, look at the sky, etc. Jesus is present in these moments when our flesh engages everyday reality. As in Bergoglio's farm, care for creation can serve as a locus for us to live 'a spirituality of the flesh.'

This summer I took this ideal of 'prayer in the flesh' and decided to put it into practice. I invited three young men and a guide to undertake a pioneer pilgrimage for the Year of Mercy. In May, we left from Rome on foot and walked to Krakow for World Youth Day on July 25th. We walked every day for two-plus months covering over 2000 km (about the distance from Washington, DC to Dallas, TX) along a 'scenic route' through Italy, Austria, Germany, Czech Republic, and Poland. This pilgrimage was certainly an experience of *prayer for* creation: we prayed together and alone, during the day as we walked and stopped at shrines, during Mass and adoration. But we also *prayed in* creation: through the beauty of landscapes, incredible churches, and art– and *prayed in* the flesh: through blisters, injuries, weight loss, sores, and muscles, and even the in gratitude for the incredible food.

I can share one important lesson I learned: patience. You just have to learn patience on a trip like this because everything just takes so long! It would take about two days by car and two hours by airplane to cover the same distance we walked in two months. Impatience, resentment, complaints, weakness, stoicism, grumbling, and long faces don't really get you any further any faster. All you can do is put on a good face in the morning and walk your 'today' until tomorrow comes. If it rains, you take a break. If it rains all day, you get wet. If you go without dinner, you try to get a big breakfast the next morning. You learn that God is in charge and He doesn't always give us what we want, but always gives us what we need. And this... requires... patience. A long pilgrimage like this is a masterful lesson in patience that is learned because it is lived in the flesh.

The day I arrived in Krakow I gave a presentation about *Laudato Si'* and our pilgrimage for the Year of Mercy. I was lucky to have a brief chat with a cardinal, and he asked me only one question: "So what did you learn about mercy?" After bumbling around for an answer a word came forth from the inside: "patience." Mercy takes patience, the kind of patience of the father who is waiting, for years, for the prodigal son to arrive. "Merciful like the Father" is also "Patient like the Father" – not anxious or stressed waiting, but hopeful waiting. It's not the impatience of the prodigal son, nor the resentful and fake patience of the older brother. These are not the rhythms of mercy.

This was the lesson I learned through my 'prayer in the flesh' and the one God had in store for me. But Jesus has many lessons in store for each one of us. And, we don't have to go on long journeys to distant places to find them, but only look at the concrete world around us in the circumstances and places we live, and decide to do something incarnate with our prayer: celebrating a meal with friends, gardening, spending an evening in the park with the family, cleaning the garage, or going for a walk. These of course must be accompanied by encounters with Jesus Christ at Mass, adoration, confession, biblical reading, prayer groups, etc. But the Pope's emphasis lies in the invitation for us to bring our prayer into the flesh.

REFLECTION

PAUSE:

Spend a few minutes in silence, settling into a comfortable place where you can allow your body to relax. If there are a few areas that you are still tight or tense, notice that and take a couple deep breaths to release the tension and offer it to God.

PONDER:

- After reading the story, what struck you the most?
- Were there some themes you resonated with?
- Themes that you noticed a resistance within you?
- I invite you to read Job 12:9-10

Which of all these does not know that the hand of the Lord has done this? In his hand is the life of every creature and the breath of all mankind.

What word or phrase stood out for you?

PRAY:

Talk with God about it; then, ask God what he would like to say to you about it?

PRACTICE:

Together with God, consider one concrete action step you can take today based on what you heard, read, or experienced during this time.

CLOSING PRAYER (OPTIONAL OR YOUR OWN):

Dear Lord,

Thank you for your efficacious gift of creation. Help us to be stewards of your wonderful handiwork which has been entrusted into our care. We ask for your protection of our land, of our seas, and most of all, of our lives. May we remember your Divine handprint originating from before the beginning of time to the end of time and to forgive us when we have intervened and cut short the gifts of nature and of life itself. We ask for your mercy and open ourselves to receive the gift of your loving presence always. In Jesus' Name, Amen

*Ricardo Simmonds: Italy, Australia, Germany, Czech Republic, and Poland

JOURNAL ENTRY

_____

_____

_____

_____

_____

_____

_____

_____

_____

_____

_____

_____

_____

_____

_____

_____

APPALACHIAN
MOUNTAIN ROAD*

∞

"Peace I leave with you; my peace I give to you. I do not not give to
you as the world gives. Do not let your heart be troubled and do not
be afraid." John 14:27 (NIV)

One Sunday, I was driving through rural North Central
Pennsylvania along Route 6, from my father's house back to
my home in the Philadelphia suburbs. Dad had died unexpectedly
the previous November, and on that particular February weekend, my
sister and I began the long, laborious task of preparing our childhood
home to sell.

Weighted down with grief, sifting through so many memories was mentally and emotionally draining, and I was relieved to take a break from it and return home. On my way back to Philly I took a route that added ninety-minutes to an already long five-hour trip, which may seem like an odd choice given my exhaustion, but I was desperately in need of the scenic route that day.

It was late morning, and I was lost in a haze of thought as the thick grey winter cloud cover started to give way to isolated patches of blue. As I crested a hill somewhere west of Wellsboro, the zenith revealed a picturesque scene. I looked on a beautiful snow-covered valley almost completely untouched by human civilization. Courtesy of the emerging sunlight, water dripped from girthy maple branches in the foreground, while a grove of evergreens set back from the road held a heavier frosting. This escarpment on the edge of Pennsylvania's slice of the Appalachian Mountains may not rival the breathtaking vistas of more jagged ranges, but it was nonetheless so striking that I felt compelled to pull over to fully appreciate the vivid setting. I took a moment to pause and just breathe in nature.

This unplanned interlude felt like a gift arriving right when I really needed it. The view was something not simply appeasing, but consoling; not only calming, but eminently peaceful; not just good, but Godly.

I sat there and soaked in the quiet beauty. I thanked God for the much-needed gift.

In trying times, I often pray for greater perspective, and for gratitude. As I grow older, these seem more and more to be two sides of the same coin. Having faith doesn't mean our troubles magically disappear, but prayer can help us to begin to understand how God works through those trials to draw us closer. The motto of Peak Encounter Ministries is, "Through Creation, the Creator and created meet," and I hadn't truly appreciated that wisdom until that roadside moment. Hiking a trail, canoeing down a river, and even taking a spontaneous break on a road trip through a wintry forest can all be opportunities to experience nature as one of many signs that God is always holding us in the palm of His hand.

What troubles you? The stress of the pandemic and physical isolation? The back-to-school worries of being a student, or a parent, or a teacher? The divisive political atmosphere? In our deepest hearts, we seek not just an absence of conflict, but true peace. This is a peace the world cannot give; only God can.

REFLECTION

PAUSE:

Spend a few minutes in silence, settling into a comfortable place where you can allow your body to relax. If there are a few areas that you are still tight or tense, notice that and take a couple deep breaths to release the tension and offer it to God.

PONDER:

After reading the story, what struck you the most?
Were there some themes you resonated with?
Themes that you noticed a resistance within you?
I invite you to read John 14:27

"Peace I leave with you; my peace I give to you. I do not give to you as the world gives. Do not let your heart be troubled and do not be afraid."

What word or phrase stood out for you?

PRAY:

Talk with God about it; then, ask God what he would like to say to you about it?

PRACTICE:

Together with God, consider one concrete action step you can take today based on what you heard, read, or experienced during this time.

CLOSING PRAYER (OPTIONAL OR YOUR OWN):

Dear Lord,
Grant me the perspective to understand the depths of Your love.
Grant me the gratitude to see Your hand always at work in my
life. May I always remember to seek you in pausing, in the silence,
and in the wonders of Your Creation. In Jesus Name, Amen.
*Jeff Klein: Wellsboro, Pennsylvania

JOURNAL ENTRY

RUSTIC CABIN*

∞

"For God alone, O my soul, wait in silence, for my hope is from him."
Psalm 62:5 (ESV)

Raised in Minneapolis proper, I am very much at home in the bustle of all the city. But I was also raised with a balance that I recognize to be unique, a full month of every childhood summer was spent on the border of Minnesota and Canada at our family cabin – and a genuine cabin with no roads, no electricity, no phone, no running water.

As a girl who always listened to music, called friends daily, and didn't leave the house without curling her hair, one would think I dreaded that month away from "civilization." In reality, I anticipate each trip and its impact on my body and soul remains evident as an adult.

The playground God provided includes the lake for swimming, canoeing, kayaking, or water skiing, the woods for hiking, hide-and-go-seek-tag, or obstacle courses, and the rocks for scrambling, sitting with a book or lying on our backs. Inevitably, even with family all around, there were pockets of quiet.

It was in that quiet of the woods that I learned to simply BE with God. My senses soared as I gazed at the wonder of creation, listened to the wind blow through the trees, smelled the sweet air, felt the sun and the water on my skin, sat by the fire with my family – and it was where, as a teenager, I said to God in that silence: "I suppose I could actually talk to You...."

As a disclaimer, I must say this is not an assertion that a return to nature can or should replace physical churches, the gathering of communities, or formal prayers. I do recognize, however, that God intended to point our eyes to Himself through His original cathedral (a.k.a. all the beauty of the earth) and that my time in the woods gave God an opportunity to intimately draw me in.

The woods are where I learned to receive His most simple gifts – in body and soul – even before I started comprehending the glory of union I was receiving in the Eucharist. The Theology of the Body, a document written by Saint Pope John Paul II, stands on the basic premise that we are made in the image of God. To teach us what that means, God deigned that we – and all creation around us – would be a set of analogies and glimpses into Himself. Creative energy, order, beauty, and the five senses to pick up on it. Humans have an intellect that operates on a different plane than animals do, with the freedom to love, body-soul unity, and desires for love and timelessness. All these describe the way God intended us to be while simultaneously showing us some little insight about the Trinity.

In our culture, beauty has been twisted and silence is all too rare. We don't take time to acknowledge God and we avoid the big questions. For many, there is a gap between the physical and spiritual realms, one is attended to while the other is brushed aside. It has been my experience, especially with the onslaught of electronics invading every second of our time, that unplugging and heading to the woods is the best remedy (of course, second to Mass and Eucharistic adoration) for remembering who God is, who we are created to be as body-soul persons, and how we are called to love like God loves. Hopefully, it goes without saying that we must remain conscious and participate in this great story for which God created us.

REFLECTION

PAUSE:

Spend a few minutes in silence, settling into a comfortable place where you can allow your body to relax. If there are a few areas that you are still tight or tense, notice that and take a couple deep breaths to release the tension and offer it to God.

PONDER:

- After reading the story, what struck you the most?
- Were there some themes you resonated with?
- Themes that you noticed a resistance within you?
- I invite you to read Psalm 62:5

"For God alone, O my soul, wait in silence, for my hope is in him." What word or phrase stood out for you?

PRAY:

Talk with God about it; then, ask God what he would like to say to you about it?

PRACTICE:

Together with God, consider one concrete action step you can take today based on what you heard, read, or experienced during this time.

CLOSING PRAYER (OPTIONAL OR YOUR OWN):

Dear Lord,
Thank you for the gift of silence. Often, I can resist what silence has to offer because it is not as familiar, or perhaps, I am afraid of what will come up in this undistracted time. Help me to carve out a few minutes each day to be silent as a way to rest, to ponder, to be open to your voice. In Jesus Name, Amen!
* Jen Messing: On the border of Minnesota and Canada

JOURNAL ENTRY

_____

_____

_____

_____

_____

_____

_____

_____

_____

_____

_____

_____

_____

_____

_____

_____

_____

_____

Dark Stroll*

∞

"You will not fear the terror of the night,
nor the arrow that flies by day..."
Psalm 91:5-6 (NIV)

The night walk is the ultimate experience. The place of meeting for the thinkers and the talkers alike. Big or small; happy or sad; alone or together, it is a private meeting for those who seek purpose and validation. You will never feel less lonely in your life. There is just one condition—honesty. Being honest with yourself and with Him. This is not for the faint of heart as it can be terrifying at first but exhilarating by the end. The moon brings to light a world not seen by the sun. Its ambient glow, resembling that of the Holy Spirit in your chest, bringing to life things you didn't know existed.

WALK ON...

You come to a crossroads, whether it be on your journey or in your conversation with the Creator. In either situation, we are to analyze possible threats. For example, cares, sins, and bad habits. Come up with a plan. Where to turn, where to go. Choose to take God with you. Allow yourself to be guided by Him, as He has walked these roads many times before you. He will get you through this even if you don't know how.

WALK ON...

The moon is centerfold, a piece of beautiful decor hanging in the midnight sky dotted with dull clouds, drowned out by a sea filled with stars. You can almost feel their pull, their magnificence. They float in black nothingness making their presence known, demanding that they be seen despite the darkness. There isn't a star out there that during its creation He wasn't expecting you to see on this very night at this exact moment. Each sparkle, every newfound light is for you on this night. He loves creating, and He loves sharing. He wishes to share what He loves with you. Join Him. Give Him your attention and let Him see your inner stars, the ones that shine when things become dreary, and desolate. The stars that make you...well...you!

WALK ON...

A drop...and another...So the rain begins. A shower becomes a torrent in the ground is gone. Below you is only a reflection, lit by the still present crescent moon. The fine details aren't present, only your silhouette. Is this water coming to take... or to give? To destroy...or to create? Often these things are not as they seem at first and can be misunderstood. We must take care not to get too focused on the self-perceived notion that we know God fully. We don't understand Him fully. You now stare at the vibrating reflection of yourself for answers. The truth is, we can't even fully understand ourselves at times. That's OK, we live, and we learn. Now look up and smile. Embrace the rain, dance with the lightning, and sing with the thunder. God does not create to waste, and all is created with intention. The intention is for you. Accept the gift.

WALK ON...

At long last, the coming of the light to shine upon tired eyes and a weary smile. A new day, a new beginning. A fresh breeze, and the grass comes to life. The trees shake off their statuesque outer shells, and the colors are born again. The fire lit sky comes to the earth like a mother rescuing an infant from a nightmare. Perfect harmony.

The night walk is more than exercise and is more than silence—it is pure privacy between you and the Grandest One in the universe and you're always greeted upon ending a night walk by a roar of applause only nature recognizes. Take care not to wait long before joining Him again, as everything you are to see He has waited since the birth of time to show you.

REFLECTION

PAUSE:

Spend a few minutes in silence, settling into a comfortable place where you can allow your body to relax. If there are a few areas that you are still tight or tense, notice that and take a couple deep breaths to release the tension and offer it to God.

PONDER:

- After reading the story, what struck you the most?
- Were there some themes you resonated with?
- Themes that you noticed a resistance within you?
- I invite you to read Psalm 91:5-6

"You will not fear the terror of the night, nor the arrow that flies by day, nor the pestilence that stalks in the darkness, nor the plague that destroys at midday."

What word or phrase stood out for you?

PRAY:

Talk with God about it; then, ask God what he would like to say to you about it?

PRACTICE:

Together with God, consider one concrete action step you can take today based on what you heard, read, or experienced during this time.

CLOSING PRAYER (OPTIONAL OR YOUR OWN):

Dear Lord,
Help me to recognize you have had your hand in my life from my conception. Give me the grace to become aware that in all pivotal moments in my life, you have been present. With your illuminating light, infuse hope and healing where darkness abounds within my soul or within the relationships

surrounding me. Open my eyes to celebrate the victory that is in you, even when I don't see it. You are transforming me through those moments, developing my eyes to see you with a clearer vision. In Jesus Name, Amen!
*Sean Cavanagh: Bald Head Island, North Carolina

Journal Entry

_____

_____

_____

_____

_____

_____

_____

_____

_____

_____

_____

_____

_____

_____

_____

_____

_____

_____

_____

Walk Through the Seasons*

∞

"I will meditate on your works"
Psalm 145:4-6 (NIV)

" With Christians, a poetic view of things is a duty. We are bid to color all things with hues of faith, to see a divine meaning in every event" (Saint John Henry Newman). This quote reveals the key for the interpretation of all reality. We are a mysterious harmony of flesh and spirit. We are not merely of this earth, but have, as it were, one foot in eternity. We are in fact, an embodied thirst for the Infinite! This truth explains the ache we feel in the face of beauty, or creation, of music, love, and even suffering and death. It defines the pull in our hearts for immortality. In the words of Pope Benedict XVI, "Genuine beauty... gives humanity a healthy 'shock!' it draws him out of himself, wrenches him away... from being content with the humdrum – it even makes him suffer, piercing him like a dart, but in so doing it 'reawakens' him, opening afresh the eyes of his heart and mind, giving him wings, carrying him aloft" ("Shockingly Beautiful").

This poetical view, this vision that pierces through flesh and bone to reveal the spirit, this is the lens through which we are called to perceive the world! It is a specifically Catholic vision, a sacramental vision; it shows us that the things we can see, and smell, and taste and touch are in a certain sense sacramental signs, visible realities housing invisible truths. In a certain sense, everything is a sacrament. Nature itself is a book that speaks of God. Shakespeare once wrote that we should, "find tongues in trees, books in the running brooks, sermons in stones, and good in everything" (*As You Like It*).

The truth about God "breathes" through creation, for He made it, and most of all through the creation of man and woman, made for life-giving love in the image of the Trinity. The body is a sacrament that proclaims the Mystery of God! It speaks, and our spiritual life, which animates and is knit inextricably to our physical life, is crowned with the gifts of intellect and will. But our reason and so much of what it gathers from the senses is like a rocket that can propel us only so high. Like a trapeze artist letting go, faith grasps our hands from above when reason can barely touch the fingertips. This is the path of the human person: to harmonize both faith and reason. To look with human eyes, to scrutinize with our intellect, and using reason like a launch pad, to leap into Love.

This is a journey, as Pope Francis alludes to in his recent work, *Laudato Si'*: "The universe unfolds in God, who fills it completely. Hence, there is a mystical meaning to be found in a leaf, in a mountain trail, in a dewdrop, in a poor person's face. The ideal is not only to pass from the exterior to the interior to discover the action of God in the soul, but also to discover God in all things."

The temptation today, as it always has been, is to divorce the marriage of the invisible and the visible. To close the door to the Other World and simply grasp and gather to ourselves what we can for the here and now, because, as they say, "You can't take it with you." But a sacramental vision would assert that, if it's God you are seeing through it all, you CAN take it (or better, Him) with you! As Venerable Fulton

J. Sheen once wrote, "To materialists this world is opaque like a curtain; nothing can be seen through it. A mountain is just a mountain, a sunset just a sunset; but to poets, artists, and saints, the world is transparent like a window pane–it tells of something beyond... a mountain tells of the Power of God, the sunset of His Beauty, and the snowflake of His Purity" (Sheen).

The poetical view is the holistic view. It is harmony. It is not a reduction, a less than, but an illumination, a *more than*. We see more than what meets the eye! As Pope Benedict XVI says, "Parables interpret the simple world of everyday life in order to show how transcendence occurs in reality itself. Hence, it is only by way of parable that the nature of the world and of man himself is made known to us" (*Principles of Catholic Theology*).

Creation itself is a kind of sacramental encounter that bridges worlds, connects and encounters the Divine and the human, and if we open up our senses, we sense this truth. We feel it in our bones and in our blood. In the immortal words of John Denver, "You fill up my senses!" I'm certain I'm not alone in this. In feeling this feeling, this ache, that seems to always intensify when my personal favorite season rolls around. When October comes. This ache has many names; orenda, sehnsucht, weltschmerz, wanderlust, hiraeth, šākan. It's a simultaneous dissatisfaction with the world and a soul-deep attraction to the signs and wonders contained within it. It's that numinous pull at the human heart towards something beyond ourselves, beyond the rim of the world. It first swelled up in me and came brimming over in unexplainable tears probably around the 5th grade. It was more than those back-to-school September blues. This pang was stretching into winter. It left my heart feeling hollow. "We shall be haunted by a nostalgia for divine things, by a homesickness for God which is not eased in this world even by the presence of God" (Houselander).

I'd feel it haunt me sometimes as I'd speed past the blueberry fields on my paper route, or walk about the rust-red cranberry bogs that surrounded our little town growing up. The writer Walker Percy once wrote that when we're 10 years old, this longing stirs, and it never goes away.

Author James K.A. Smith says, "The way to the heart is always through the body" ("Online Conversation"). I felt that truth in my bones. Those melancholic streams leaked into my heart through the sound of a cold October rain washing over leathered leaves, and in the ghost rattle of branches in November. I'd look up and see them yawning, scraping at the grey autumn sky and I'd feel that existential weight. Even as I write this, a whisper of the feeling returns, and maybe you, as you're reading, are feeling it too.

The comedian Louis CK refers to it as that "empty forever empty," courageously naming it on a late-night episode of Conan O'Brien. "You know what I'm talking about?" he said, leaning towards Conan. "I know what you're talking about," replied the fellow comedian, suddenly serious. We are all, it would seem in the words of the late Msgr. Lorenzo Albacete, "an incarnate why." We have a walking thirst. An embodied ache.

Now I'm not a fan of horror stories, scary movies, or the like. I remember hating having to read Edgar Allen Poe's "Tell-Tale Heart" in high school and the "Fall of the House of Usher." But I do know what all the creepy masks are attempting to mask. What is Halloween, in the secular sense, but the cultural naming and claiming of this hollow in our hearts? It's the stone over the tomb. It's the creaking door opening into abysmal darkness. The long hallway that keeps stretching further away from us even as we timidly step closer. And we step into it simply because we truly are this "incarnate why." Though we shout to the actors on the movie screens "Don't open it! Don't go down there!" still, in this ache, we secretly want to know. Is there something there? What is it?

The author C.S. Lewis travelled the dark road of atheism for years. I say dark for this system of unbelief because it's the self-willed shutting off of any transcendent light that might illuminate this dark passageway of our existential angst. Atheism refuses to look for any teleological dimension to life, any inherent meaning. But Lewis felt the haunting still.

"It is always shocking to meet life where we thought we were alone. 'Look out!' we cry, 'It's alive!' Therefore, this is the very point at which so many drawback – I would have done so myself if I could – and proceed no further with Christianity" (Lewis).

Thankfully, he did step onto that road that "goes ever on and on," and followed it bravely until he came to terms with the haunting of his heart. Curiously, it happened too on an autumn day, walking the trails at the university with his Catholic friend, J.R.R. Tolkien. As they felt that October chill, and those same leathered brown leaves swirled about their feet, they discussed mythology, a favorite study for them both. Tolkien told his friend these fables they both loved were not lies "though breathed through silver" as Lewis claimed. They were whispers, allusions, hauntings if you will, of a great Spirit at work in the world. The ancient stories held a glimmer of truth, and that truth is, this Spirit is real. Just as real as that initial fear that comes when we realize we are not alone in a darkened room. This talk with Tolkien was the beginning of the end of Lewis's atheism.

Now back to our hearts. What should our posture be as we enter into these hollow and hollow places within us? Let's recall the way to the heart is in fact through the body, through the senses, and God so designed the world to come to us that way. In making us body-persons He is using all of these things to speak to us, to teach us, to love us and to draw us to him. With prayer and discernment of spirits, we must feel it all, even as Christ did, and we can long with him for the Father in those dark vigils on mountain tops and olive groves and craggy hills.

> Let everything happen to you: beauty and terror.
> Just keep going. No feeling is final.
> Don't let yourself lose me.
> Nearby is the country they call life.
> You will know it by its seriousness.
> Give me your hand.
> – Rainer Maria Rilke, "Go to the Limits of Your Longing"

REFLECTION

PAUSE:

Spend a few minutes in silence, settling into a comfortable place where you can allow your body to relax. If there are a few areas that you are still tight or tense, notice that and take a couple deep breaths to release the tension and offer it to God.

PONDER:

- After reading the story, what struck you the most?
- Were there some themes you resonated with?
- Themes that you noticed a resistance within you?
- I invite you to read Psalm 145:4-6 (NIV)

"One generation commends your works to another; they tell of your mighty acts. They speak of the glorious splendor of your majesty – and will meditate on your wonderful works. They tell of the power of your awesome works – and will proclaim your great deeds."

What word or phrase stood out for you?

PRAY:

Talk with God about it; then, ask God what he would like to say to you about it?

PRACTICE:

Together with God, consider one concrete action step you can take today based on what you heard, read, or experienced during this time.

CLOSING PRAYER (OPTIONAL OR YOUR OWN):

Dear Lord,
Thank you for all you have created. You created all the sunrises, the sunsets, the mountains, the seas, the living creatures, the dry and fertile land, and most of all, you breathed life into me!

Help me to see all the beauty you have created as a sign of your generous love, a love that reaches towards us, inviting us into a deep relationship with you. In Jesus Name, Amen!
*Bill Donaghy: Self-Reflection

JOURNAL ENTRY

BUS TO UMBRIA *

∞

How beautiful upon the mountains are
the feet of him who brings good tidings
Isaiah 52:7 (RSV)

Adventure is not my middle name. My parents had great foresight there! Though a college athlete and a runner today, when it comes to a risky physical undertaking, I'm happy to run in the other direction. The rush that some experience with the potential for physical danger baffles me. Actually, the potential for any physical discomfort baffles me. My husband enjoys telling friends and strangers that my idea of camping is spending a night in a hotel that doesn't have room service. (I still don't understand why such a hotel exists!)

Don't get me wrong; I'm not a total wimp. I've whitewater rafted down the Snake River in Wyoming—twice! Hiked in California's Kings Canyon National Park—alone! And took the Polar Plunge in Anchorage, Alaska—albeit, in the middle of August, on a cruise ship, into a heated pool. But I did it. I may not seek adventure, yet I've learned working in the vineyard of the Lord allows adventure to find me, in many ways! All three action-packed experiences were the result of sharing the Gospel.

On a beautiful fall morning, Teresa Tomeo and I arrived in Rome. As leaders of the *WINE & Shrine Women's Pilgrimage through Italy*, we always fly into Rome a few days before our pilgrims to give ourselves some "downtime." This allows us to be well-rested when the women arrive. Thus, we planned a relaxing first day—a leisurely stroll, a nice *pranza* (lunch) with some *vino*, and a little sightseeing. But our ways are not the Lord's ways, and soon our relaxing day turned into a thrill-seeking adventure as we found ourselves on a strenuous hike and in the middle of a drug deal that ended with a James Bond-like car chase through the streets of Roma!

Knowing we'd be in Rome, a friend asked if we could drop something off for a priest at the *Angelicum*. Underestimating the distance from our hotel to the *Angelicum*, we decided to walk. Hours later, sweaty (and a bit stinky), we reached our destination. We clandestinely met with Father outside the gates and delivered the drugs. Well, actually, they were vitamins, but somehow pretending we were in some epic Hollywood thriller made three hours of enduring the hills of Rome more doable! What happened next, however, could have come right out of a movie.

Worn out from the walk, we opted for a taxi ride back to the hotel. Any taxi ride in Rome is potential for physical danger, but this one took that to the extreme. At speeds comparable to NASCAR, Mario Andretti (our name for him) tore through packed cobblestone roads, missing pedestrians, and Vespas by inches. He took one turn so sharply that Teresa and I slammed into one another. It was then that we told each other how much we enjoyed working together, lest we didn't make it back to the hotel alive.

God keeps those who work for Him on their (sometimes nicely pedicured) toes and grants blessings along the way. As Teresa and I talked during *cena* (dinner) that evening, we realized our exhausting and terrifying day in Rome, filled us with much joy and laughter, and gave us ample reasons to be grateful and give glory to God. A peaceful night>s sleep offered another reason to praise God!

The next morning, well-rested, we met forty-five jet-lagged pilgrims and boarded a coach bus to Assisi. On day two, we set out for Norcia, the home of Saints Benedict and Scholastica, nestled in the rolling hills of Umbria. Our bus rides are filled with prayer, spiritual teachings, lessons on the Motherland (as Teresa calls it), chatter, laughter, music, and singing. We had just finished a teaching on Scripture, followed by some praise and worship music (Italian-style, i.e., loud), and the ladies were settling in for a little rest. In the front two seats, Teresa and I were chatting away when the bus came to the peak of a hill. Instantly both of us gasped as the spectacular portrait of the Umbrian hillside stretched out below us. The beauty was breath-taking: tears filled in my eyes. For the first time, in probably forever, Teresa and I were both speechless. I looked at her and saw tears streaming down her face. We started laughing uncontrollably, entirely overcome by the beauty of God's creation and filled with tremendous gratitude that He gave us the blessing of this mountaintop experience.

Sometimes working in the Lord's vineyard can take its toll, and the Lord knows that, for, He refers to us a "laborers in the vineyard," not frolickers. (Luke 10:2) But we can take great comfort knowing that when Jesus commissioned us to go to all nations and proclaim the Good News, He also assured us He would be with us... always. (Mathew 28:20).

I have no doubt that the Lord gives His evangelists mountaintop experiences—the energizing thrill of an adventure, the uncontrollable laughter with a friend, the spectacular beauty of creation—not only as encouragement along the journey but as a glimpse into the greatest adventure that awaits those who scale all obstacles before them to bring the Good News of salvation to the world, Heaven

REFLECTION

PAUSE:

Spend a few minutes in silence, settling into a comfortable place where you can allow your body to relax. If there are a few areas that you are still tight or tense, notice that and take a couple deep breaths to release the tension and offer it to God.

PONDER:

- After reading the story, what struck you the most?
- Were there some themes you resonated with?
- Themes that you noticed a resistance within you?
- I invite you to read Isaiah 52:7

"How beautiful upon the mountains are the feet of him who brings good tidings, who publishes peace, who brings tidings of good, who publishes salvation, who says to Zion, "Your God reigns.""

What word or phrase stood out for you?

PRAY:

Talk with God about it; then, ask God what he would like to say to you about it?

PRACTICE:

Together with God, consider one concrete action step you can take today based on what you heard, read, or experienced during this time.

CLOSING PRAYER (OPTIONAL OR YOUR OWN):

Lord, help me recognize the gifts you have equipped me with to share the Good News. Give me the courage and the wisdom to share my love for You with those I meet along the journey. Thank You, for bringing me with You on this great adventure! In Jesus' Name, Amen!

*Kelly Wahlquist: Norcia, Italy

JOURNAL ENTRY

SCUBA DIVING*

∞

Before I was born the Lord called me; from my mother's womb,
he has spoken my name.
Isaiah 49:1 (NIV)

From as far back as I can remember, I imagined I was a mermaid. A beautiful, weightless princess of the sea gliding through crystal blue waters among colorful fish, dazzling coral, and breathtaking creatures of all shapes and sizes. Unafraid in my underwater kingdom – I was at home. My hair swirled around me like a silky cloak as I basked in the rays of the sun filtering through the surface to reach the world below.

Water has always provided me with a sense of peace, freedom, and calm. It is where I feel most alive and connected to our Creator. I found that when I needed a place to pray, to seek solace, or simply to breathe deeply throughout my life I would head to the nearest shoreline and instantly feel grounded again. My mermaid dreams and affinity with the sea were a part of life, an innate desire inside of me, leading me in everyday choices such as how to spend my spare time, what books to read, subjects to study, where to vacation and where to call home, and even what pets to choose.

A few years ago, as a fluke I signed up for a scuba certification class. My boyfriend Scott was already certified and enamored me with stories from the deep.

Scuba certification consists of eight weeks of classroom time, learning about safety and procedure as well as time in the pool putting the lessons into practice. We learned that a successful dive depends not only on vigilance with safety procedure, but that your life depends on your ability to trust and have faith in God and your dive buddy. Scuba is a partnership sport. You and your dive buddy rely on each other when sixty feet underwater. The knowledge that I am held in God's powerful hands at all times provides a freedom and shield from panic and fear that can grip you in a heartbeat.

Upon earning my certification, Scott and I traveled to a rustic dive camp in Turneffe Atoll, an hour, and a half off the mainland of Belize, to explore the second largest barrier reef in the world. This was my moment to put the practice, trust, and faith to the test and literally dive in! My heart fluttered and stomach churned with anticipation as the boat headed out for the first dive. The beauty of the crystal blue water surrounding mangroves was almost too much for me to process. I found myself thanking God over and over for access to His masterpiece that is Belize. On cue, we slipped on our fins, masks, and scuba gear and took the plunge. Instantaneously, my entire life felt transformed. I was made for this! The deeper I swam the greater I felt my connection to God. Surrounded by bright pink, yellow, and electric blue coral teeming with life, the heart-to-heart dialogue with our Lord was natural, continuous, and powerful. Without words, we spoke. He led me, just like the mermaid I dreamed to be, to abundant treasures I never knew existed and certainly don't deserve.

I was weightless as I slowly waved my hands in front of me, drifting along the currents with nurse sharks and rays scouting along the sandy bottom, enormous schools of colorful fish surrounded me like a tornado kaleidoscope. I twirled playfully alongside enormous sea turtles and pursued moray eels springing from the shadows like wavy ribbons. I never felt so complete and fulfilled, so satisfied and overwhelmed by God's love as in that moment.

The Lord's hand was in mine in the depths, guiding me and protecting me. I was not afraid, and I trusted him fully as he shared with me this natural and surprising gift buried deep in my heart only to be discovered once I tapped into who I was created to be. The Lord so clearly called me to this moment, patiently provided hints of what would make my soul sing, the most profound gift I have ever received. The gift of being known, cherished, and recognized as his child.

REFLECTIONS

PAUSE:

Spend a few minutes in silence, settling into a comfortable place where you can allow your body to relax. If there are a few areas that you are still tight or tense, notice that and take a couple deep breaths to release the tension and offer it to God.

PONDER:

- After reading the story, what struck you the most?
- Were there some themes you resonated with?
- Themes that you noticed a resistance within you?
- I invite you to read Isaiah 49:1

"Before I was born the Lord called me; from my mother's womb, he has spoken my name."

What word or phrase stood out for you?

PRAY:

Talk with God about it; then, ask God what he would like to say to you about it?

PRACTICE:

Together with God, consider one concrete action step you can take today based on what you heard, read, or experienced during this time.

CLOSING PRAYER (OPTIONAL OR YOUR OWN):

Dear Lord,
From the world's beginning, with your loving and gentle gaze, you dreamed of my existence. Help me to always remember that you delicately and deliberately created me in the moment of conception in my mother's womb. May I live life knowing my identity as a son or daughter made in your image, meant to impact the world for good, resting in the hope that is found in you. In Jesus Name, Amen!

* Elizabeth Hoisington: Turneffe Atoll, Belize Barrier Reef

JOURNAL ENTRY

Star Gazing*

∞

"You have searched me, Lord, and know me."
Psalm 139: 1- 4 (NIV)

It was probably the thousandth time in my life I stared at the stars; however, it was the first time I thought of the stars as more than just dots in the sky. Suddenly, I was immersed in God's enormous creation, imagining the stars, millions of light-years away and had an interior sense that life was so much bigger than the realities I had right in front of me. I can't explain it, but God was shifting my perspective in that moment. I suddenly felt that my circumstances were much smaller in the grand scheme of life. In that moment of awe and wonder of the Divine Architect, I tried to stay grounded in that present, practical reality, sinking my feet into the ground in front of me.

God stirred something within my heart that night as I marveled at Arcturus high in the sky and Antares twinkling brightly. Acturus was much more noticeable with its soft, reddish-orange colored, soft texture. That day marked the growing interest in wanting to study Astronomy.

That summer, I watched as many videos as I could and in the fall, I enrolled in an astronomy class offered at my high school. Part of this investigation was certainly driven by my scientific mind with particular interest in Math, Chemistry, and Calculus, as well as a general desire to learn. Astronomy just seemed to fit neatly into what I already liked.

The fuel which kept me pursuing the stars was the spiritual sensations I received that summer night and many nights that followed. I experienced an interior movement of increased

reverence, realizing the grandeur of God and my place within it. While looking up at a sky full of stars, rather than a quick glance as I walked by, I began to consider God's guiding hand directing me to my proper place within His creation. When one takes in the grandeur of the stars, it is impossible not to be humbled.

Even the magnitude of the sun is daunting; then consider Betelgeuse, 270,000 times bigger and brighter than the sun. Anyone with even the slightest crack in his or her wall of pride will find God busting through with each glance at the cosmos. I realized that there were a lot more important things in life. It reduced my ego-inflated sense of self-importance. Reflecting on it now, I recall the summer of my Junior year in High School, I attended a Youth Conference. Saturday night tended to be the most powerful nights. We had Eucharistic Adoration, spending time before the Blessed Sacrament. As Catholics, we believe that Jesus is fully present body, soul, and Divinity in the Eucharist. I rested deeply in God's presence there for a while, then wandered off outside to a hill nearby to look at the stars. I felt a deep peace and trust as I felt God's hand in my life. I wanted to give my life totally over to him!

After being humbled, however, I was flooded with an enormous sense of dignity and my value from the stars. I would often think about the billions of other stars exactly like our own with planets quite similar to the Earth. However, it was in our simple solar system in a minor spiral arm of an ordinary galaxy that God breathed His Spirit and made man after His own image. Among all the incredible nebulae,

supernovae, and black holes in the universe, I am the crown jewel of
God's creation. Even in their incredible, colorful, mysterious beauty,
we are His biggest prize (HM – most Beloved?)

Although the stars are farther away that the human mind can
fathom, the night sky serves as a mirror for me, and among the celes-
tial bodies I see myself with great clarity. I am microscopic, a drop in
the bucket, less that a grain of sand on the earth compared to the whole
of creation. I can sometimes subtly become preoccupied with myself,
breezing through a day without checking in with people and asking
them about their day or missing an opportunity to do a kind thing.
Despite how I often behave, I am not the center of the universe or my
own master. Even so, each time my eyes meet the stars, God reminds
me that I am worth more than the most beautiful, heavenly objects,
and He whispers His love for me.

REFLECTION

PAUSE:

Spend a few minutes in silence, settling into a comfortable place where you can allow your body to relax. If there are a few areas that you are still tight or tense, notice that and take a couple deep breaths to release the tension and offer it to God.

PONDER:

- After reading the story, what struck you the most?
- Were there some themes you resonated with?
- Themes that you noticed a resistance within you?
- I invite you to read Psalm 139:1-4

"You have searched me, Lord, and you know me. You have known when I sit and when I rise; you perceive my thoughts from afar. You discern my going out and my lying down; you are familiar with all my ways. Before a word is on my tongue you, Lord, know it completely."

What word or phrase stood out for you?

PRAY:

Talk with God about it; then, ask God what he would like to say to you about it?

PRACTICE:

Together with God, consider one concrete action step you can take today based on what you heard, read, or experienced during this time.

CLOSING PRAYER (OPTIONAL OR YOUR OWN):

Dear Lord,
Thank you for giving us tangible reminders in creation that help us to shift our perspective. Through the beauty of a star lit sky, may we remember that we have been made for more

than this earthly life. Help us to see your eternal vision for all of humanity, most especially how I might live it out in my everyday life. In Jesus Name, Amen!
*Mickey Fairorth: Philadelphia Suburbs, Pennsylvania

JOURNAL ENTRY

Hot Air Balloon*

∞

"But the Advocate, the Holy Spirit, will teach you all things."
John 14:26 (NIV)

I thought it would be fun to ride a hot air balloon while visiting
Jackson Hole Wyoming! Little did I realize getting up at 4:30 AM
was part of the equation. While it was still dark, the balloon team
ignited a billowing, blazing, hot fire. The fire expanded the balloon,
reorienting the basket and balloon upright. We were invited to climb
in and ready ourselves for takeoff. This gargantuan flame was intimidating, the flame was just above our heads! Of course, being me, I
blurted out, "this can't be safe, has anyone ever scorched their hair
from the fire?" The pilot just laughed and said, "no, we need it to keep
the balloon in flight. It is the "engine" that keeps us going in the right

direction!" With a chucked, I eased a bit and enjoyed soaring over green covered plantations, hills, and valleys as the blowing wind carried us. The fire was our ally, leading the way to our final destination safely.

We have all had times when we attempted something we thought may be fun, exciting, and even courageous. Sometimes, before the "big event," a gripping fear can overcome us, causing us to doubt or decision, and we're tempted to walk away, even if it's for the benefit of others.

Let's take a look at how God handled this type of situation. On Pentecost, the twelve apostles were in the Upper Room for ten days, fearful for their lives! They just experienced the brutal death of their Lord. In Jesus' discourse before he died, he promised they would not be alone. He would send the Advocate, the Holy Spirit, who would be with them. While in the Upper Room, Jesus appeared and "breathed" on the apostles to receive the gift of the Holy Spirit. Then, "They saw what seemed to be tongues of fire that separated and came to rest on each of them. All of them were filled with the Holy Spirit." (Acts 2:3-4) It was from that point on, the apostles had the courage to move out of the Upper Room, and commitment carried out the Great Commission, sharing the Good News of Jesus Christ. His promise that he would be with them fulfilled!

When I am asked to speak at an event with over 100 people, before-hand, I can be tempted to become anxious, self-conscious, and fearful that everything I prepared for may float out of my head in an instant, wondering if I will be perceived as a fool. Maybe I won't articulate my words well, share a teaching in a way that may seem confusing, or just plain all over the place. By God's grace, if I am aware of this false perception and name it, and say "Come Holy Spirit" a few times, the anxiety dissipates. I begin to feel courageous that Our Lord is with me. Then, looking around, in God's mysterious ways, he gives me a surge of love for those I am serving and I hear the words, "I have equipped you in this particular time, in this particular place, to impact this particular group of people, with your particular life experience, to share My love with them." For the apostles, they had a particular mission to share the Good News as well. How do you experience the fire of the Holy Spirit in your life?

REFLECTION

PAUSE:

Spend a few minutes in silence, settling into a comfortable place where you can allow your body to relax. If there are a few areas that you are still tight or tense, notice that and take a couple deep breaths to release the tension and offer it to God.

PONDER:

- After reading this story, what struck you the most?
- Were there some themes you resonated with?
- Themes that you noticed a resistance within you?
- I invite you to read John 14:26

"But the Advocate, the Holy Spirit, whom the Father will send in my name, will teach you all things and will remind you of everything that I said to you."

What word or phrase stood out for you?

PRAY:

PRACTICE:

Together with God, consider one concrete action step you can take today based on what you heard, read, or experienced during this time.

Dear Lord,
When we are open to receiving you through the power of the Holy Spirit, we know you lead us, even when at times, it seems we are too saddling up for a wild ride! Help us to remember your promise that YOU are always with us on our journey! When we seek your guidance and protection, You promise to be with us always. In Jesus' name, Amen
*Heather Makowicz: Jackson Hole, Wyoming

JOURNAL ENTRY

BACKPACKING*

∞

> "Yet whatever gains I had, these I have come
> to regard as loss because of Christ."
> Philippians 3:7 (NIV)

G rowing up, I had the love of hiking instilled in me by my dad. I read a lot about nature and hiking, especially about hiking the Appalachian Trail. I sensed I'd experience a profound meaning in accomplishment if I completed the entire 2,190-mile trek. Also, I just wanted to be able to separate my college experience from whatever was going to come my way in the future.

I went in the spring of 2016. I planned my hike for five or six months. I didn't train for it. I mean, I did some hiking, but I didn't train. I did a lot of research because I'd never backpacked before. I spent time putting together a pros and cons list, and I had to really know myself well because there is a lot of gear out there. For example, do I buy a whole rain suit, to protect me from the rain, or get wet anyway from sweat.

I got myself into the mind frame of a backpacker, knowing that I would need to depend on myself and the things I had on my back to survive. I made my decision for gear and they served me well because I loved pretty much every single piece of gear I selected. I didn't have to dump a lot of stuff along the way to lighten my load. Nothing was wasted!

I was going into the unknown! Because I didn't have that experience, It took me six months.

As I trekked through the mountain trails I saw things that people left like pots and pans.

I started at Amicable Falls State Park in Georgia. I had trained there with my dad and we hiked the approach trail, which is technically not part of it. I practiced using my equipment before I set out on the trail.

The first day I arrived at the peak where the trail begins.

I set up my campsite that night and cooked dinner. As excited as I was leading up to all of it, my heart sank. I want to do it all! But I started to think, "I've never done this before, I don't know what I'm doing, this is going to take forever!"

I stayed awake all night! I thought there was a mouse scratching at my tent, and when I woke up the next morning, it turned out to only be a stick rubbing up against my tent!

"Oh, boy, this is real, and scary!" I knew it was going to be hard! I had the decision to make. Will I stop now or keep going? Luckily, my dad accompanied me in the beginning and kept me afloat when I needed the positivity. Also, there were others who started the same time as me with different experience levels. They hit the same trail, the same weather, and the same mountain, that was a big earning especially when the mountain doesn't care if you succeed.

Once, a hiker told me that the mountains are great levelers or equalizers. What you want and how far you're willing to stretch yourself to get there will also humbles. Many people go into it thinking that they know everything and are so prepared. But there is always going to be something unexpected, whether it was the weather or a water source running dry. There's anxiety provoking, problem solving along the way.

My mantra. "one step at a time, one step closer to Katahdin," which is the end of the trail in Maine. This parallels life where you feel very anxious about your future, about the unknown. You don't know how you're going to get there or how well you're going to get there.

You kind of forget to live in the moment and enjoy where you are and to remember, it takes lots of little detailed work to get to that point. Saying things like, one step closer boosted my confidence and reminded me what the goal was.

Having to get up in the morning on the trail, pack up everything, load up your whole pack, literally your packing, unpacking, and repacking all day even just to get to your lunch. It's a small bag, but you have to have a slot for everything. If I take unnecessary stuff, I make it heavier. It was vital to be intentional.

If it rained I had extra dry clothes. That's part of my preparedness.

I knew at the end of the day, even though it's a hassle to set up a tent in the rain, l knew I would get to have a warm meal, I would get to dry off, get into warm clothes and be in my tent at night.

I think of one of the biggest things I learned was discipline and self-confidence. Having endurance when things are uncomfortable, challenging, as well as physically and mentally demanding. But I guess it's having that fortitude, really sticking with something when it's not easy. That was huge!

On my very last day of hiking I was maybe half way up Mount Katahdin in Maine. I bumped into somebody going the opposite direction. He was actually starting a southbound through hike and I was just finishing my northbound hike. So, he was going to be hiking all the way to Georgia. I was taking a break and having a snack on a rock and he was all energetic in the beginning, I recalled how it was for me the first day too. Boy, how much things have changed!

I picked up my backpack and continued on the trail. Shortly after, I was within sight of the sign at the top of the mountain that says Mount Katahdin. This was a neat thing for me to see because on my first day, I got to the top of Springer Mountain and Chemical Falls, Georgia and I was totally overwhelmed. When I was inside of the Katahdin sign, I saw that guy again that passed me earlier. He was on his way down the mountain to really start his southbound hike and his demeanor totally changed. He made it to the top and realized that he had to walk all the way to Georgia. It's extremely overwhelming and I knew that feeling just by the look in his eyes! I could say, wow, I have been there! It was kind of amazing. All those little steps closer to him brought him closer to his goal. I wanted to say, "You can do it! Just keep moving."

* I reflected on how I am so different now than when I started. Seeing him on the trail was like I'm seeing a mirror of myself, innocent to the trail ahead.

REFLECTION

PAUSE:

Spend a few minutes in silence, settling into a comfortable place where you can allow your body to relax. If there are a few areas that you are still tight or tense, notice that and take a couple deep breaths to release the tension and offer it to God.

PONDER:

- After reading the story, what struck you the most?
- Were there some themes you resonated with?
- Themes that you noticed a resistance within you?
- I invite you to read Philippians 3:7-8

"Yet whatever gains I had, these I have come to regard as loss because of Christ. More than that, I regard everything as a loss because of the surpassing value of knowing Christ Jesus my Lord. For his sake, I have suffered the loss of all things, and I regard them as rubbish, in order that I may gain Christ."

What word or phrase stood out for you?

PRAY:

Talk with God about it; then, ask God what he would like to say to you about it?

PRACTICE:

Together with God, consider one concrete action step you can take today based on what you heard, read, or experienced during this time.

CLOSING PRAYER (OPTIONAL OR YOUR OWN):

Dear Lord,
Thank you for giving me so much. Help me to shed anything that may distract, tempt, or cause me to drift away from you. You know what is most essential in my life. Your abiding presence is enough for me. In Jesus' name, Amen
* Trix: The Appalachian Trail, New Hampshire to Georgia

JOURNAL ENTRY

_____

_____

_____

_____

_____

_____

_____

_____

_____

_____

_____

_____

_____

_____

_____

_____

_____

_____

_____

Canyoneering*

∞

"Be strong and courageous. Do not be not be afraid; do not be discouraged, for the Lord will be with you wherever you go."
Joshua 1:9 (NIV)

About five years ago, my husband and I went on much-needed
time away. We had the opportunity to go to the beautiful Zion
National Park in Utah–truly God's country, and a childhood dream
come true. There, we were able to re-experience some ways that united
us in the first place 25 years ago, namely, outdoor adventures!

One of the days, I signed us up for canyoneering, which consists of
hiking, rock climbing, stemming, and jumping from one deep crevice
to the next. Though I felt God calling me that year to conquer fears, I

knew this would be no small feat! It took everything to step out and try something new!

The red rocks were made of sandstone, occasionally causing me to lose my grip. I deeply appreciated the thick treads on my hiking boots that found a way to stick to the sides of the grainy, jagged rocks. Thank God, too, for my helmet and backpack, filled with gear to keep me safe on that sweltering 95-degree day.

After climbing to the top, I saw the mountain across from us was a gorgeous sight. But I couldn't take it in very long. A wave of tremendous fear washed over me as I peered over the edge and there was only one way down—rappel down the 200-foot-cliff!

Contrary to my natural instinct for self-preservation, to begin the descent, I was told to lean back on the ropes as far as I could, away from the edge of the cliff into...umm...nothing.

My feet wouldn't budge. I started to sweat, shake, and tighten my muscles. Paralyzed, I told myself, ' '*There is no way I am going to do this!*"

I felt trapped. I couldn't go back, and I couldn't go forward. But I knew I couldn't stay here forever either.

I took a deep breath, said the words that have gotten me through the toughest of times before, "Come Holy Spirit," leaned back on the cradle of my harness, and took my first jump down the steep cliff.

With each jump, I acknowledged my fear and pressed through with courage and trust that I would make it down to the bottom. Bouncing off the cliff felt both insane and incredibly fun, like bouncing on a springboard, only sideways.

I reached the bottom in 15 minutes. I thanked God for holding me safely in His arms as I surrendered to Him.

REFLECTION

PAUSE:

Spend a few minutes in silence, settling into a comfortable place where you can allow your body to relax. If there are a few areas that you are still tight or tense, notice that and take a couple deep breaths to release the tension and offer it to God.

PONDER:

- After reading the story, what struck you the most?
- Were there some themes you resonated with?
- Themes that you noticed a resistance within you?
- I invite you to read Joshua 1:9

"Be strong and courageous. Do not be not be afraid; do not be discouraged, for the Lord will be with you wherever you go."

What word or phrase stood out for you?

PRAY:

Talk with God about it; then, ask God what he would like to say to you about it?

PRACTICE:

Together with God, consider one concrete action step you can take today based on what you heard, read, or experienced during this time.

CLOSING PRAYER (OPTIONAL OR YOUR OWN):

Dear Lord,
We may not always know the future, but I take consolation in the ways you have already pulled me through in life. Help me have the courage to rely on, to lean back on your grace, knowing you will catch my fall. Thank you for these opportunities of growth and trust. In Jesus' name, we pray. Amen.
*Heather Makowicz: Snow Canyon State Park, Ivins, Utah

JOURNAL ENTRY

ROCK CLIMBING*

∞

"The Lord himself goes before you...do not be afraid"
Deuteronomy 31:7-8 (NIV)

When I took up rock climbing I had two immediate goals: to overcome a lifelong fear of heights, and to get my mind off my former boyfriend of four years.

None of my friends climbed, and I had almost no experience. I joined an indoor climbing gym, invested in shoes and a harness, and proceeded to make a fool of myself as I struggled up the walls, belayed in the early days by a series of obliging, if skeptical, strangers.

I remember panicking at the top of the boulder cave, which is an area of short climbing walls without ropes. I was probably only eight feet above the thick padded mats, but I felt on the very edge of death.

"Help," I squeaked. A woman spotted my graceless fall, and I skulked homewards. I think I avoided the gym for over a week to nurse my wounded pride.

Another time, I spent a heart-pounding, throat-clenching, stomach-turning quarter of an hour pasted to the wall as my partner grew impatient below. "Just. Stand. Up!" she declared in exasperation. I finally figured out that a tiny foothold no more than one square inch in size was enough to bear all my weight on a single toe. That breakthrough took me to the top of my first 5.8-graded climb. To put that in perspective, 5.8 is the often-lowest grade of climb available in many of the gyms.

Through blood, sweat and tears, at last I was learning. More importantly, I made friends. There was Caitlin, Emily, Nick, Ginny, Paul, Lindsay, Henry, Rob, Josh, and many others. I soon knew that I could show up at the gym any day of the week and expect a belay. A void in my life was filling up.

As the weather warmed, opportunities to climb real rock abounded. I clambered all over the cliffs either side of the Potomac River, checked out Annapolis Rocks, and delved into the disused quarry in Birdsboro. The real deal was a long weekend I spent with four other climbers in the New River Gorge of West Virginia.

That adventure was my first opportunity to set an outdoor climb. Many established climbs have bolts driven into the rock where climbers thread their rope through quickdraws for safety. Someone has to serve as the "rope gun," ascending the rock face first to clip the rope into the bolts and anchors so the rest of the party can climb on top rope. This is called "setting" a climb. I had been practicing it indoors, but still felt intensely nervous.

Henry, who belayed and mentored me in the gym, promised that he had the perfect route in mind. After a winding hike down into the densely wooded gorge, he showed me to the base of a 95-foot cliff and pointed out the route.

With a cold knot in my stomach, I slowly pulled on my harness, checked, and double-checked each strap, tied into the rope, checked, and double-checked my knots, had Henry triple-check each one, counted out my quick draws and arranged them on my gear loops, reluctantly tied my shoes, and took an unnecessarily long swig of water.

I barely noticed two guys hurrying past us, still in their harnesses and climbing shoes. One of them was gripping his left hand with his right.

I had more immediate things to think about. At last I turned to face the cliff. The first bolt where I could hang a quick draw and gain the safety of a belay was about sixteen feet high. That's sixteen feet of vertical rock where my only protection from a fall would be my own skills and judgement. Beyond that first bolt, there were ten more. If I lost my grip at any point between them, I would fall back below my previous clip before Henry on belay could catch me. Then I would have to re-climb the stretch that had just bested me.

Slowly, I began to climb, placing quick draws and clipping in as I went. Each neat "Snap!' of a carabiner around my rope gave me a sigh of relief, but always short lived. There was a single carabiner hanging on the fourth or fifth bolt. These "bailer biners" are a sure sign that the last person to attempt the route gave up and was lowered from that point, sacrificing a valuable piece of gear in her retreat.

That was about 35 feet above the ground. I almost stopped. "You okay?" Henry called up to me. "I have so much fear right now," was my truthful reply. I heard Rachel barely suppress a sympathetic chuckle. "I know. But you got this! You're doing great!" she yelled.

By that point in my climbing career, I had learned just two crucial techniques: Breathe and look up. I completed the rest of the climb with my eyes resolutely towards heaven, breathily whispering over and over again "Be not afraid. I go before you always."

At long last, I reached the top of the cliff, clipped my rope into the anchors, gleefully yelled "Take!" and sat back into my harness with a deep sigh. Cheers and applause erupted from my comrades nearly one hundred feet below. Only an act of God could have brought me that far. I fairly floated back down to earth, lowered expertly by Henry, and cushioned by a great billowing wave of triumph.

Next up was Jonathan, climbing swiftly with the constant security of the rope I had anchored. But when he reached the top, he gave a startled shout. "Chiara! Why didn't you mention the snake?!"

"What snake?" I yelled in reply.

"This huge copperhead on the last ledge before the anchors!"

I had no answer. In my intense focus, I hadn't even noticed it. Fortunately, Jonathan was able to stay safely out of its venomous reach.

Later, we met other climbers just down river. "Didja see those two guys hiking out earlier?" a woman asked us. "One of 'em got bit by a copperhead on a high ledge. Look before ya reach!"

We all let this cautionary tale sink in. The gorge was too narrow and too deep for a quick rescue. No wonder those climbers had seemed in a rush to get out! His life depended on it. I thanked God fervently for my own escape.

Again, and again I find myself in uncharted waters, or at unprecedented heights where I cannot see what lies ahead, yet I am called to step beyond what I think I can do. Sometimes I just need wings. It is then that Christ says "Be not afraid. I go before you always."

REFLECTION

PAUSE:

Spend a few minutes in silence, settling into a comfortable place where you can allow your body to relax. If there are a few areas that you are still tight or tense, notice that and take a couple deep breaths to release the tension and offer it to God.

PONDER:

- After reading the story, what struck you the most?
- Were there some themes you resonated with?
- Themes that you noticed a resistance within you?
- I invite you to read ...Deuteronomy 31:7-8

"Then Moses summoned Joshua and said to him in the presence of all of Israel, "Be strong and courageous, for you must go with his people into the land that the Lord swore to their ancestors to give them, and you must divide it among them as their inheritance. The Lord himself goes before you and will be with you; he will never leave you nor forsake you. Do not be afraid; do not be discouraged.""

What word or phrase stood out for you?

PRAY:

Talk with God about it; then, ask God what he would like to say to you about it?

PRACTICE:

Together with God, consider one concrete action step you can take today based on what you heard, read, or experienced during this time.

CLOSING PRAYER (OPTIONAL OR YOUR OWN):

Dear Lord,
Sometimes it is hard to stand up for what is right. Please
give me the courage to do your will when I sense the actions I
experience around me can feel cold, dark, and far away from
your presence. Give me the gift of discernment in knowing
when I am to speak and when I am to be silent and just listen.
If after praying, and the time comes to speak, fill me with your
presence and give me an internal "knowing" that you have
prepared the space to address these situations before I even
arrive. In Jesus' name, Amen
*Chaira Cardone: New River Gorge, West Virginia

JOURNAL ENTRY

MOUNTAIN CLIMBING*

"Suffering produces endurance, and endurance produces character,
and character produces hope, and hope does not disappoint us."
Romans 5:3-5 (NRSVCE)

I look for fun, crazy, and challenging things to do. Since Mount
Kilimanjaro was on my bucket list my adventure partner and
I decided to go. We climb and hike often. The doctor excluded my
partner, who also is my wife due to the effect the extreme altitude
would have on her asthma, so I contacted some friends. At sixty-nine,
most of my friends are at least sixty and have enough trouble getting
out of bed in the morning!

I just said, "the heck with it, I'll do it by myself." With my wife's
encouragement, I signed up to go January 2-16, 2020, with Tusker

Trail, a group out of California. They've put together Kilimanjaro adventures for at least thirty years and have a medical group on staff. Planning that far in advance gave me about a year to get ready.

The preparation and anticipation of going gave me joy. I walked from five to ten miles a day at Valley Forge, since they have a lot of pretty steep hills. I got myself in shape. I've always been in relatively good shape, but to climb Kilimanjaro, I needed to put in some extra effort.

I participated in a Bible study group who had a visit from a priest who is the rector at a seminary in Tanzania. I shared with him that I plan to climb Mt. Kilimanjaro. This priest exclaimed, "that's in my backyard! My seminary is in a town called Arusha. It's only 30 miles from Moshi where you will stay to climb Kilimanjaro

I arrived early and visited the seminary. My time with these incredible African seminarians was as good, if not even better experience than to hike Mt Kilimanjaro itself.

The first day of the climb I connected with two nice couples from Australia, both in their late 40s.

I signed a document before the climb and noticed about 40 signatures on the page and checked to see if anyone was my age. Nope! By far, I was the oldest guy!

The first day we climbed a steep incline of nine thousand feet with no problems at all. I Felt great! Strong!

The next day we're at twelve to thirteen thousand feet. We continue circling the mountain at fourteen thousand feet to acclimate before we summit at nineteen thousand feet. So, we're going up and down, up, and down. I was on the mountain for nine days before heading to the summit that last day.

There were five of us hikers with approximately twenty guides. Every day they would help put the tents up and knock them down while singing and performing an African dance.

One of my great memories was waking up in the morning, coming out of my tent, looking up, with the feeling you could touch the top of the snow-capped mountain. You look the other way and you're looking down at the clouds. The majesty of God permeates the mountainside.

Towards the last couple of days, increasingly, I began to feel a bit different, lightheaded. I continued to climb. The last day we were to ascend the summit with a cold blizzard forecasted for the next morning. It was 20 degrees and with a wind chill below zero.

The guides said they didn't think I should go any further with the coming blizzard. That October, they lost two or three guides in a blizzard. I never made it to the top.

My next goal, when I'm seventy-five, is to try to get up there again. I'm happy I got up and into those heights, even while not feeling great, because I continued to press on. I did not give up.

Having those experiences, every journey you have, you've got to take the first step. Many people don't want to step forward or are scared to take the journey. Don't take a journey by yourself, God is with you.

I like to end each day with a challenge, both an internal spiritual challenge as well as a physical challenge.

REFLECTION

PAUSE:

Spend a few minutes in silence, settling into a comfortable place where you can allow your body to relax. If there are a few areas that you are still tight or tense, notice that and take a couple deep breaths to release the tension and offer it to God.

PONDER:

- After reading the story, what struck you the most?
- Were there some themes you resonated with?
- Themes that you noticed a resistance within you?
- I invite you to read Romans 5:3-5

"And not only that, but we also boast in our sufferings, knowing that suffering produces endurance, and endurance produces character, and character produces hope, and hope does not disappoint us, because God's love has been poured out into our hearts through the Holy Spirit that has been given to us."

What word or phrase stood out for you?

PRAY:

Talk with God about it; then, ask God what he would like to say to you about it?

PRACTICE:

Together with God, consider one concrete action step you can take today based on what you heard, read, or experienced during this time.

CLOSING PRAYER (OPTIONAL OR YOUR OWN):

Dear Lord,
Thank you for giving me free will in this life to share in all the goodness you have created! As a pilgrim on a journey in

this life, show me your light and your lead in everything I do. When I encounter challenges, give me the grace to remember to "check in" with you to see if this is an obstacle you've invited me to move past. If it is, I ask for you to give me fortitude to press on, knowing the final destination will be the ultimate prize, uniting with You in heaven. Jesus Name, Amen!

*James Delaney: Mount Kilimanjaro, Tanzania

JOURNAL ENTRY

_____

_____

_____

_____

_____

_____

_____

_____

_____

_____

_____

_____

_____

_____

_____

_____

_____

_____

_____

_____

WHITEWATER RAFTING*

∞

"But one thing I do: forgetting what lies behind and straining forward to what lies ahead, I press on toward the goal for the prize of the upward call of God in Christ Jesus."
Philippians 3 :13-14 (ESV)

I was with one of our instructors recently. He's a good friend of ours. He shared something very powerful, connecting whitewater rafting and navigating through obstacles, most especially rocks. One day, he was observing his wife, Cristen Zimmer, preparing to navigate away from this rock about twenty feet downstream. He knew that she had plenty of time to slightly turn her boat and get away from the obstacle.

This was a valuable teaching moment. He asked her, "what are you looking at right now?" She said, "Well, I'm looking at the rock that

I want to avoid!" He replied, "No, look where you want to go!" She followed his instructions and narrowly escaped hitting the rock. After her first near miss she focused on where she wanted to go and avoided every rock to complete her ride with a smile and dry clothes.

Metaphorically, if we look at a sin that we know turns us away from God, we can go about life saying, "I want to avoid that sin." What I found is that when I continue to stare at that sin I don't want to commit and try everything to avoid stumbling. Instead, when I turn towards holiness, there is a shift in perspective from turning away from sin to turning towards virtue. When I focus on holiness, I'm no longer turning inward, but outward.

So, if I'm focused on treating my kids with kindness and not yelling at them, or treating my wife with respect and love, I can choose to just focus on what I'm not doing well, which can be discouraging, or I can choose to focus my mind and heart on looking toward virtue. With God's help, there is hope and worry fades away.

Interesting antidote, my wife went from feeling like she would never become a good raft guide to eventually becoming one of the only female Class V commercial guides in Colorado and the US Women's National Championship team captain and guide and she and her team won a Bronze Medal in 2 world cups, one in Ecuador in 2006 and one in New Zealand in 2012.

REFLECTION

PAUSE:

Spend a few minutes in silence, settling into a comfortable place where you can allow your body to relax. If there are a few areas that you are still tight or tense, notice that and take a couple deep breaths to release the tension and offer it to God.

PONDER:

- After reading the story, what struck you the most?
- Were there some themes you resonated with?
- Themes that you noticed a resistance within you?
- I invite you to read Philippians 3: 13-14

"But one thing I do: forgetting what lies behind and straining forward to what lies ahead, I press on toward the goal for the prize of the upward call of God in Christ Jesus."

What word or phrase stood out for you?

PRAY:

Talk with God about it; then, ask God what he would like to say to you about it?

PRACTIZCE:

Together with God, consider one concrete action step you can take today based on what you heard, read, or experienced during this time.

CLOSING PRAYER: (OPTIONAL OR YOUR OWN):

Dear Lord
Thank you for creating me in Your image, including the desires of my heart. Help me to dig deep with you to explore and respond from those deepest desires. Renew my mind to remember those desires, those yearnings were created on purpose. They were created to lead me back to you to which all of life flows.

Please give me the grace to understand that you fill our heart's deepest desires and rather than to run away from them, to run towards You, who renews all things, most especially us, your most beloved daughter or son. In Jesus Name, Amen!
*Cristin Zimmer: Buena Vista, Colorado

JOURNAL ENTRY

Entry #16

Surfing Hehe Nalu (Mountain Waves)

Go Big or Go Home | The Day of Coragio
"Lead me to the Rock that is higher than I" Psalm 61:2

Bear Speaks

I heard the surf report say it was the biggest day in over forty years. Just then the phone rang, it was my youngest son Joshua. "Dad Crazy Todd is taking Jeremiah (my oldest son) out to tow him into these waves with his jet ski. It's big Dad, the biggest I have ever seen." This was it. This was the day Jeremiah had dreamed of and had prepared for his whole life. With a big lump in my throat, I grabbed my keys, jumped in my hummer and headed up the forty-minute drive to the North Shore of O'ahu from my home in Waikiki. Adrenaline was juicing through me.

My heart sank as I drove through the pineapple fields and topped the rise and saw in the distance a heavy mist from the big surf as "Hehe Nalu" (mountain waves) built up and broke. They were so big that they seemed to break in slow motion as they rose and rose and then threw out. When it is big I count the seconds between the time the wave pitches and when the lip impacts the water in front of the wave. It seemed like time stood still.

I got to the harbor at Haleiwa. "Where is he Josh?"

"I don't know Dad." Came his worried reply. "They headed out past the harbor buoy and then they were just gone." I looked out towards where the buoy was supposed to be, but it was nowhere to be seen. It was submerged under the big building surf.

I had surfed waves at the famous big wave surf break called Waimea Bay that only breaks when the face is at least twenty-four feet, but the younger surfers now had taken it to a whole new level. When the waves get so big that we just cannot paddle fast enough to catch them on our big wave elephant gun boards, they switch over and get towed in by powerful jet skis. These waves were out of control. It was big. The Coast Guard later said that they had tracked a hundred-foot wave on their radar that day on the north shore.

Would Jeremiah live through this day? He was as ready as he ever would be and he had the great waterman, Big Wave Surfer and one of my best friends Crazy Todd Robertson handling the jet ski. They both had trained for years for a day like this "Big Wednesday." Jeremiah and I would practice holding our breaths for the duration of the sunset, we would paddle our board on the open ocean for twenty or more miles and we would paddle a half mile out in front of my home in Waikiki and dive down twenty feet deep and grab a boulder and run under water. When he was just eight years old he started bombing down big hills on his skateboard. I knew he would not back down.

I prayed.

As darkness began to fall I saw a lone Jet ski out beyond the harbor indicator buoy waiting for a lull. Finally, it jetted fast into the harbor, out running a monster wave. As it got to the boat ramp and the engine cut off, I could see that Jeremiah's countenance was one of exhilaration and satisfaction. Crazy Todd yelled out "He got the Juicy One. Biggest I have ever seen ridden. Taller than any coconut tree."

"Jeremiah!" I yelled "How was it?"

"It was Big Dad." he smiled back. "It was Big." He was basically just speechless.

It has been over ten years since that big day. With the prompting of Heather the other day, he just seemed to open up and let it all out, as he talked story (as we say in Hawaii) about that day.

Jeremiah Speaks
"As we jetted out of the harbor and around Puena Point, it was already late in the day. We were met by several other jet ski teams that were coming back in. "How was it?" Todd shouted.

They shouted back "It's too big! No one can ride today."

Todd opened up the throttle and yelled back to me with his usual crazy laugh. "I know just the spot–Outside Alligators." The other teams turned around and followed us back out to watch and to be there for a rescue if needed. They idled their skis in a deep channel as Todd and I continued for another two miles before he eased back on the throttle. We began to get our bearings and wait for the next big set.

Then, one of the biggest waves I had ever seen, started to build up on the horizon. Todd towed me out to meet it and then turned to run with it as it slowly began to build up under me. As it began to *peak*, he jammed full speed and dropped in over the crest, then he turned hard back out to sea as he whipped me into this monster wave. It continued to build under me as I dropped down its face. It was a good practice run but I wanted a bigger one, so I made a hard bottom turn and kicked out the back of the wave. Todd cruised by and I grabbed the handle on the huge boogie board, that we call "the sled," on the back of the jet ski and pulled myself and my surfboard on it as Todd headed back out. Todd knew why I had kicked out. He turned and asked me; in his pigeon, "You like to go big?"

I sat on my board looking out to sea for a long pause then looked up and said. "Yes! It's a good day to die." When you surf big waves, you have to decide ahead of time that you are going to die. But then you must trust in your jet ski partner with the hope that he can get to you and you pull you by the hook by the back of your neck on the vest and onto the sled and then revive you. If you can't commit to this you should not surf big waves. There is nothing worse than the wipeout that comes when you hesitate or second guess your courage at that critical moment of dropping in.

We slowly cruised back and forth slowly making our way out to the deeper part of the reef and waiting for the next set of monster waves. It was apocalyptic. We had about five minutes to get ready. They were coming for us. I jumped off the sled with my surfboard with the tow rope and Todd pulled me up out of the water. It felt unreal as we headed out to meet these mountain waves. They rolled under us, each one bigger than the one before. They were lifting us and lifting us and then letting us back down on their back side. We kept waiting for the Biggest One of the set.

Suddenly, Todd said "We go." He jetted the ski and I was pulled up and out of the water. As the mighty wave came towards us we turned towards shore almost ad full throttle trying to match its speed. It was like being on the back of a monstrous whale as it's back rose up and up out of the water. The mound below built and built into a mountain. It kept building more and then it began to rise up more steeply and began to *peak*. As it felt the reef below, it rose up more steeply it was time to drop in. Todd opened up the throttle to full speed jetting over the lip and then turned and whipped me down into the face of this monster.

Suddenly I was alone. You are always alone in Big Surf. You and your guardian angel are the only one you can rely on at that moment. I kept trying to get my bearings. It was strangely quiet. I kept dropping down the face, but because the wave was still building, I was taking an elevator ride up. The silence became more intense. I kept waiting for the sound of the wave breaking behind me. I was totally alive. This wasn't a death wish. It was a wish to truly live. I was totally living in that moment. I remembered a picture of Crazy Todd riding a Big Wave so big that the Helicopter filming him was below him. It was that big and getting bigger and steeper. I felt the fins and rails of my board holding the line but I felt that they could break loose at any

moment I would just free fall and tumble down the face of the wave. The wave crashed below me and I could see that the impact zone was no man's land fifty, sixty no more than eighty feet below me. .

I leaned in and dug my rail and began to careen down the line across the face of the wave. Then I heard it. It was a distant thunder that kept growing closer and closer as the wave kept exploding behind me as I flew down the line. Now it sounded like the loudest crackling thunder I had ever heard. I could hear God's voice in that apocalyptic wave. The Book of Revelation says that his voice is "a voice like many waters." The bible says that God defeats his enemies with his Word, with his voice. My advice. Don't mess with God. Don't take him for granted. He is more wild and dangerous than this wave. My Dad's creed is "The most radical thing you can do in life is abandon yourself to the wild adventure of God's will." Being in God's will is where all the fun and the action is but you must not trifle with God.

The was peeling now as I rode more than a mile down along its face. I could see that I would need to ride another half a mile at least to get to a spot to kick out without it swallowing me up. I was locked in for the ride of my life. I was fully committed from the time first dropped in. This was not a time for second thoughts or doubts. Just absolute focus on every moment. Living every moment in the moment.

The memory flashed through me how since I was a child I had a magazine picture of a surfer riding a big wave on my wall. When I was only eight, I would practice bombing down big hills on my skateboard. I knew one day that it would be me riding giant waves. Now here I was. I was riding a wave bigger than anything I had ever seen in person or even in magazines or videos. The wave must be over eighty feet maybe a hundred feet by now. The thunder kept getting louder and closer as the barrel began to catch up with me. I told myself that, even though looking back for even a moment was extremely dangerous, I knew if i did not look back into the barrel of that wave that I would regret it for the rest of my life. I risked looking back and what I saw was horrifying, It was beautiful. You could stack several busses on top and besides each other in the gaping jaws of that barrel. Its colors were shocking as they went from a brilliant blue and then faded into green, to dark green and hundreds of yards deep inside the barrel of the belly of this beast it was just dark and black.

I quickly looked back in front of me and refocused my attention forward knowing I had to make that wave. I had to keep flying down along its face looking for a moment to kick out and escape like a bull rider leaping off the back of a rogue bull. It was beginning to throw. I was in the belly of the beast. I looked up at the barrel that was throwing over me now about forty feet above me. I had to make it out. If I turned and surfed to the bottom of its face it would explode on top of me. If I held the line down the face, it would only be a few more moments before it threw me cartwheeling down its face before it sucked me back up and then threw me over the falls again to be pummeled in the impact zone. Think of how heavy a bucket of water is. Now think of the weight and power of the water in a hundred Olympic size pools being dumped on your head.

There was no way out.

But then instinct took over or maybe it was my guardian angel. I leaned hard into the face of the wave grabbing it with my right hand as a pivot point and then dug into the back of my board with my back leg with all my strength and pivoted the trajectory of the board straight up forty feet straight at the ten-foot-thick falling lip that was throwing out over me. I flew straight up the face to the ceiling of the tube above me. As I was about to smash into the lip, I launched myself off my board and pushed hard with my right arm extended in a fist and tried to superman myself and punch through that thick lip.

Suddenly. I had made it.

I had shot through to the back of the wave without it sucking me backwards over the falls. I could only hope somehow Todd had been able to shadow me along the lip of that wave for that mile and a half. Then I saw him, but he did not see me. He had ridden past me and kept running with the wave. He was anticipating and hoping that I would live and pop up at some point out of the white water. Then he could jet in and get me. Whether I was alive or dead, he would grab me and pull me on the sled. He kept looking all around him.

"TODD!" I yelled "TODD! OVER HEAR!" I hoped that he would see me. More waves were coming in from the horizon. Finally, he looked back and caught a glimpse of me and flew up to me as he pulled me up on the sled behind the ski. He looked like he was seeing a ghost.

"How did you get here?"

"I supermanned it Dude! Right through the lip." I grinned back.

He laughed "But Dude," then a look of grave concern came over him "Where's my board?" It was then that I realized the leash that attached me to the board snapped. I made it through to the other side but the board didn't. He picked me up and we made a run along the foam of the impact zone and then somehow, we found it. I grabbed it as we zipped by and as I sat on the saddle behind Todd and we both quickly looked out to sea. There was corduroy to the horizon. There was an endless set of waves stacking up on each other, each one bigger than the next. There were maybe fifty waves with forty to one hundred foot faces. We were not out of harm's way yet.

It's counter intuitive. Everything screams inside a surfer to make a run for the safety of the shore, but we would have been eaten alive before we got in. My Dad and I have seen jet skis at Teahupoo in Tahiti not just exploded but actually disintegrated by smaller waves than these. Every surfer knows when the big sets roll in, you must paddle out to try to get our to sea beyond the clean-up set. We had to full throttle the jet ski to try to make it out past each successively bigger wave before it broke.

We would go so fast at the rising lip that when we made it over we would free fall back down on the other side. At one point Todd and I were both thrown off the ski. When that happens the lanyard on his wrist turns the power to the ski so it doesn't take off without us. A jet ski can get you into situations that only a jet ski can get you out of. We swam as fast as we could, jumped on and then Todd throttled as we screamed outward towards bigger and bigger surf. Finally, we are out in the relative safety of deeper water. It was starting to get darker. The sun had set.

We jetted back to the boat ramp. I waved at my Dad and my brother Josh. as we slid up to the dock the engine cutoff. Todd looked back at me. "Dude I didn't turn off the engine. We're out of fuel."

It was good. Things were very good.

Bear and Jeremiah's thoughts about life lessons:
1. God expects Christians to be bold as we step out in faith. We are not supposed to be Ned Flanders, the Simpsons next door neighbor. God is a great and powerful God. The closer we get to God, and the more we abandon ourselves to the power of his will, we will need to have our wits about and be wise and prudent. We will need to have courage because God calls us to be warriors such as times like this. Timid people

don't need prudence. They just need a couch and a bag of chips. Prudence is for the bold. Prudence is the Charioteer of the virtues.

2. Pay attention to the dreams, desires and gifts that you have. God's will for your life lies in them for he created us for a purpose. You will be sifted and your intentions purified and your skills tested and developed but then God will use you and fulfill you. You must be like Moses when he had to lay down his shepherd's rod and then "The Rod of Moses became the Rod of God."

3. When surfers paddle out, we learn to turn our back on the aina, the land, and paddle out into the deep and wait searching the horizon for a set of waves to roll in. We must learn the lesson of detachment. We must turn our back on the ever-changing temporal things and paddle out to seek the face of God, to seek things eternal and then to wait in anticipation of God moving. We "strive to enter into God's rest." We rest from our will and seek his will.

4. When we see the wave, we paddle to position ourselves in just the right spot to catch it at the *peak* of its power. When we are about to catch it, we need to paddle in with all our might. When we sense God's will, we love God back, when we strive to enter into it with all of our heart, soul, strength and mind.

5. Never turn your back on the ocean. Every year, tourists here in Hawaii get swept out to sea here when they are posing for a picture standing on the beach with their back to the ocean and a wave suddenly sweeps them out. Do not take God for granted. Respect him and honor him. He is not to be trifled with. So many people rely on God's grace to save them but never seek to be a disciple. God's grace is not cheap like that. After all it cost Jesus his life.

7. Sometimes when we paddle for a wave, we miss it. But so many times when this happens it positions us to catch the bigger better wave. So, it is in your spiritual walk. We may seek to move in what we sense is God's will but then it does not seem to work. Then suddenly we realize that what we thought was a failure was just God positioning us in his will.

8. From the shore, when people see big surf they lose all sense of the dimension of the waves. It is only when they see the surfer and the wake of the board along its face that they realize just how great the waves are. So, it is as Christians, as we move in God's will, people should see how great and good God is.

9. Surfers know to always cut back along the face of the wave to ride as close to the power of the *peak* as possible. Sometimes, after a big drop on a big wave, we start going so fast along its face that we outrun the power center of the wave. We can end up stalling and then the wave catches up to us and eats our lunch. We need to be careful as Christians, that what we begin in the Spirit we do not end in the flesh in our own strength and power. We must always cut back in prayer and seek the lord's will, timing, power and grace.

10. Of course the ultimate rush for a surfer is to be locked so deep in the barrel, that the surfer is totally hidden. That is how it should be with us and Christ. We should be hidden in him. As we serve the Lord people should not see us, they should just see Christ.

11. There are moments of surfing when we are totally locked in and living only for that moment. That is how our life needs to be for God is 'Yahweh' (I am who am). He lives in the eternal now. Jesus said "Before Abraham was. I am.' Learn to be totally alive in the moment and seek the reality of God with you.

12. When I was on that big wave I looked back. Sometimes when worry and doubt plague us or we need to re-establish our sense of direction, we just need to take a moment and look back for a moment and see how faithfully God has been with us even in the most confusing of times. He made sense of them for us and we know he has a beautiful plan for our lives.

13. Of course we can't talk about surfing without talking about big wipeouts. At times the wipeout is so big that we are held down for more than one wave and we are thrashed about and confused and don't know where we are. That is when we go into a fetal position to protect our limbs from being torn off and we go to our happy place. There is nothing we can do but

to wait for the wave to release us. Sometimes we get pushed down so hard, and so far, that we hit the bottom of the reef. That is actually a good place to be because at least then we know which way is up and we can push off from there. When we hit the bottom, and come to the end of ourselves, we tend to let go and let God. That is where we hear him knocking. That is where we listen for his "still small voice." That same one that roars like many waters. The same one that the bible says is "a voice behind us shouting. This is the way. Follow it."

14. Once we push off the bottom after a big wipeout, we swim towards the light at the surface. Even though we are getting closer to the surface, our lungs are feeling worse and worse, screaming because of the poison of the carbon monoxide building up. This is a good thing. It gives us a sense of urgency to swim hard. Then suddenly we burst through the surface. As the oxygen fills our lungs, the light seems so bright and we are so happy. This is how it is in the long dark nights of our spiritual journey. The longer the hold down, the more we are aware of the poison that we have allowed in our life and all we want to do is expel it and live in the breath of God's love and will, which by the way is the same thing. When the dark night ends, you learn to set aside the selfish agendas of a mercenary love that loves God because of what he does for you and now you learn to love him just for who he is.

15. After a surfer has a great ride, the satisfaction is so real and so deep. The people will come up to us on the beach, but they will never say "Man you were amazing!" Instead they give credit to the wave. They will say "Man that was a great wave." We want our lives as Christians to be only a hand that points to the glory and goodness of god.

16. When we turn to paddle out when a Rogue set is coming, we do not run from our fears. We turn to face them. As Jesus said "In the world you will have tribulation, but be of good cheer! I have overcome the world."

REFLECTION

PADDLE OUT AND WAIT:

Spend a few moments in silence and then take a few minutes to just pray your love for God by just saying the name of Jesus. Breath in the Aloha (in Hawaiian it means breath) of the Holy Spirit and Breath out your devotion by saying his name.

PONDER:

What struck you the most in reading the story?
What did you find a resistance to?

What do these words of King David mean to you right now in your life. "Lead me to the Rock to High to Climb and I will Climb it." Psalm 61:2

PRAY

Talk with God about it or maybe write him a short letter. What do you sense God may be telling you.

PRACTICE:

Together with God, consider one concrete action step you can take today to set you on a new trajectory in an area of your life.

CLOSING PRAYER:

Lord,
Let me know you. Let me know your will. Lord give me the power and grace to walk the path of Deep Adventure that you have for me.
In Jesus' name,
Amen

*Bear and Jeremiah Woznick, Oahu's North Shore, Hawaii

JOURNAL ENTRY

SAILING*

∞

"Do not be anxious about anything."
Philippians 4:6-7 (ESV)

If I could live anywhere, I'd choose to be "by still waters," as in Psalm 23, where the Lord our Shepherd "leads me beside still waters; he restores my soul." Nothing calms and satisfies my soul like the sight and sound of a stream, or of waves lapping the shore. Yet, water can be wild and scary, as in a storm-tossed lake or a hurricane.

The terrified disciples of Jesus were caught in a storm on the Sea of Galilee. "Don't you care if we drown?" they cried to Jesus. With a word, Jesus stilled the wind and the waves. (See Mark 4:39-41.)

I get the idea, though, that he was disappointed in them. "Why are you afraid?" he asked, maybe grumpy at being woken from his nap.

"Have you still no faith?" It seems a more mature bunch would have weathered the storm without losing their calm. They would have drawn on God's peace, the kind that "surpasses all understanding" by holding us steady *regardless* of the storms of life (see Philippians 4:6-7).

We vacationed on a lake in Vermont, and one summer my parents got us sailing lessons. I'll never forget the feeling of being in command of the boat. One hand on the tiller, the other on the line; setting the boat perpendicular to the wind and then angling the sail just right so it fills with air. If I close my eyes, I can feel the wind on my face. I can hear the hull gliding forward, sense the moment when the wind slacks and it's time to bend low, duck under the boom as it comes about, and shift to catch the breeze again.

One day my brother and I each grabbed a Sunfish and launched them into the lake, racing to where we knew we could buy ice cream at the other side. Halfway there, a wind came up. Joe grinned and zoomed past me. My rudder jerked and then I lost control, frightened of the sudden waves. The sail whipped across and knocked me off the boat. When I came up for air, all I could see was Joe in the distance, sailing steadily to shore.

I've often thought of the way Joe's sail held steady while my boat floundered as a picture of God's peace. The same wind blew both of our boats. The same waves attacked us. My eyes were on the danger, where his eyes were on the goal. And the wind that caused me so much trouble speeded him to shore.

God calmed the sea for the terrified disciples. Sometimes he'll calm the storms for us, as well. But whether he does or not: if we keep our eyes on him and trust, he can take away our anxiety and give us the kind of peace that helps us sail on through.

St. Paul knew the peace of God and told the Christians in Philippi, "Do not be anxious about anything, but in everything by prayer and supplication with thanksgiving let your requests be made known to God. And the peace of God, which surpasses all understanding, will guard your hearts and your minds in Christ Jesus." (Philippians 4:6-7)

Three things: Turn to the Lord. Keep an attitude of thanks. Ask for help! And he will guard your mind and heart with peace. Taking you "by still waters" in your soul, even if the storm still rages on.

REFLECTION

PAUSE:

Spend a few minutes in silence, settling into a comfortable place where you can allow your body to relax. If there are a few areas that you are still tight or tense, notice that and take a couple deep breaths to release the tension and offer it to God.

PONDER:

- After reading the story, what struck you the most?
- Were there some themes you resonated with?
- Themes that you noticed a resistance within you?
- I invite you to read Philippians 4:6-7

Do not be anxious about anything, but in everything by prayer and supplication with thanksgiving let your requests be made known to God. And the peace of God, which surpasses all understanding, will guard your hearts and your minds in Christ Jesus."

What word or phrase stood out for you?

PRAY:

Talk with God about it; then, ask God what he would like to say to you about it?

PRACTICE:

Together with God, consider one concrete action step you can take today based on what you heard, read, or experienced during this time.

CLOSING PRAZYER (OPTIONAL OR YOUR OWN):

Lord, thank you for being with me in the storms of life! Help me to keep my eyes on you at all times. I want to set my course by your guidance and not in reaction to the disturbance around me. Right now, I'm feeling [tell him your situation]. Please give me your "peace that passes understanding" along with the grace I need to ride the waves to you. In Jesus' name, Amen!
*Sarah Christmyer: Vermont

JOURNAL ENTRY

CAVING*

∞

"He has put eternity into man's mind, yet so that he cannot find out
what God has done from the beginning to the end."
Ecclesiastes 3:10-12 (RSVCE)

In 1992, while still in high school, my buddies and I traveled to
Colorado's, Lost Creek Wilderness area where we backpacked often.
I explored this random cave. I by no means am a caving expert, in fact,
I'm actually kind of claustrophobic.

As we started hiking down the trail, I had to pee. So, I just go over
to a bush. I start to pee, and I hear nothing hitting the ground! I pull
the bushes to the side. I discovered a hole that went to the bottom of
the river, the full 200 feet! I freaked out because I couldn't believe it!

I grab my headlamp and shine it down this hole underneath the bush the size of a manhole approximately three feet tall and two feet wide descending to the river. I find my brothers and urge them to check it out. Astonished, they exclaimed, "This is amazing!"

I had this brilliant idea of repelling the cave to check it out. I knew a little bit of what I was doing, so I tied a rope to a tree, and had a good grip of the mountain and we lowered this rope. We had two ascenders, which is a piece of climbing equipment. They are little ladders and you hook yourself to one of them. The little ladder is also connected to the rope and your harness. Your body goes up two feet, and then you rest at your waist, so your legs are free. Then, you slide your ladder up, step up, and you basically climb up the rope.

In this cavern, the size of a bedroom, we look around. Then we noticed a crack downstream from where we were. We investigate further. Towards the back of this little dark room, we noticed a little tiny hole about three feet tall and a couple feet wide. We shine our headlamps to see in this dark room. Remember, I've never been caving a day in my life and I'm kind of claustrophobic, but somehow, this experience excited me! We crawl for about twenty-five feet into the hole. Unexpectedly, it opened up into a giant room that was probably like thirty feet wide and fifteen feet tall with a stunningly beautiful, sandy beach with the little river running through it. It was just like a typical brown, sandy beach color. We were just blown away! We sat there for thirty minutes, and I took a few photos.

We believed that we were the first people there, we didn't notice any signs. There could have been somebody but the rising water could have erased the footsteps.

Where I went to the bathroom, there was no indication, no sign of anything beyond or underneath that bush, I had to deliberately check it out! I could have lost my step and that would have been it!

I never thought much about that moment until now. The spiritual aspect was powerful.

Here I am thinking that I knew the world that I was entering. I would go to college, get a job, marry, have children and there would be that same routine. After my brothers to a place where they have never been before and to recognize that there's something out there in this world that you don't even know exists. Nobody has told you it exists, excites me.

So, from a spiritual standpoint, I guess I didn't see a relationship with God as an adventure. I grew up a cradle Catholic. You go to church on a normal Sunday, do your routine, and it was never any big eye-opening experience for me.

But in that moment, at 17, in High School, my perspective changed. I was blown away at the awe and wonder, the mystery of God and how He creates beyond our wildest imagination! What's so crazy is that caving that day, I had a very powerful experience that affected me down the road. It taught me that life is adventurous!

God has so many of these untold unexperienced adventures for us, that if we ever think that life is dull, or life is boring, that it's not!

Because if you pursue life, knowing that God is there for you and that he has an amazing life for you to live, it will be an adventure!

You can live a really safe life where you don't want to step outside your comfort zone, just getting by day by day, then you might not have these opportunities that can give you a wake-up call, to invite you to further growth.

REFLECTION

PAUSE:

Spend a few minutes in silence, settling into a comfortable place where you can allow your body to relax. If there are a few areas that you are still tight or tense, notice that and take a couple deep breaths to release the tension and offer it to God.

PONDER:

- After reading the story, what struck you the most?
- Were there some themes you resonated with?
- Themes that you noticed a resistance within you?
- I invite you to read Ecclesiastes 3:10-12

"I have seen the business that God has given to the sons of men to be busy with. He has made everything beautiful in its time; also, he has put eternity into man's mind, yet so that he cannot find out what God has done from the beginning to the end. I know that there is nothing better for them than to be happy and enjoy themselves as long as they live."

What word or phrase stood out for you?

PRAY:

Talk with God about it; then, ask God what he would like to say to you about it?

PRACTICE:

Together with God, consider one concrete action step you can take today based on what you heard, read, or experienced during this time.

CLOSING PRAYER (OR OPTIONAL PRAYER):

Dear Lord,
Thank you for surprising me with many gifts you deliver to me every day, even in my regular routine. Though predictability

can be peaceful, there are times when you invite me to move beyond that comfort zone to try something new. When I step out, I step into your grace as you shine the light on the terrain ahead. Give me the foresight to look ahead with hope and the future you have set, individually tailored just for me. In Jesus Name, Amen!

*Tom Zimmer: Lost Creek Wilderness Area, Bailey, Colorado

JOURNAL ENTRY

ICE CLIMBING*

∞

"Everyone helps his neighbor, one says to his brother, "Take courage!"
Isaiah 41:6 (RSVCE)

Not many people choose to go ice climbing over New Year's in western Colorado, yet, I did! I realized the dangerous journey before me as I peered over the edge of a 200-foot cliff with a sheer wall of glass and frozen water. I walk towards the edge of that cliff, anxious about many things, namely, the ministry I decided to build in order to save souls and how Jesus took risks in His ministry.

I didn't need to be here right now! I could have been reading Latin or Hamlet somewhere with a little lamp over my book. I could be doing something that my peers would be doing, like playing cards in a warm, cozy cabin.

Instead, I am invited by my guide to begin the treacherous, unfamiliar descent. "Ready, Father?" He asked. "Step over the edge!" Testing my harness again, I questioned whether I would be up for the challenge. Seeing the hesitation in my demeanor, the guide smiled, "Are you sure?" He reminded me that if anything went wrong, he could haul me up himself, but laughingly said he would prefer not to. I ask him what could go wrong? He smiled and said, "You'll find out when you go! Just make sure you have your walkie-talkie on you. If anything goes wrong, you can signal up to me and I'll help you out. Also, make sure that you don't go all the way to the bottom because there is a considerable 25-foot gap between the bottom of the canyon and a sea of broken ice. If you land there, you can't get up."

I gulped, placed my spikes firmly into the ice and leaned back over the edge. I moved at a quick clip, repelling over the ice. If you've never been ice climbing, it's unlike anything else in this world. Ice climbing is a sport where your entire ability to get to the top lies above you, with four small spikes digging into the ice as the only points of contact holding my full weight.

Can you imagine peering up a 200-foot sky-scraper? Now, imagine that the whole building is nothing but ice. The colors reflected hues of brilliant blue and clear crystal. That's the really hard ice to decline!

When you ice climb, by necessity, you need to find the smallest, little deviation on the ice. It is there that you place your ice tool in order to get your strongest grip. Depending on the spikes on your shoes, your axe-shaped ice tool, and a steely crampon, the climber puts all of their weight as they pick their way up the surface wall of ice. Sometimes, the deviations are so small, they are unnoticeable. In that case, they have to swing the axe tool strong enough to penetrate the ice enough to get a firm grip. This can be risky, because sometimes the ice can be pried so loose that it breaks off, leaving you to either hang there, fall, or get injured by the broken ice descending down on your head! Whether these thoughts race through your mind or not, the climber has been determined to keep climbing, deliberately measuring the choices before them as they hug the slick, blue, clean, frozen water on the side of the mountain. My thoughts were full of things like, "Why in the world did I ever do this?"

Acknowledging my questions, I continued on, resolving to be courageous, and lead by example. I began to hear the young people gathering close to the edge, cheering me on as I completed the climb. On the outside, they saw this brave 42-year-old priest leading the way. On the inside, I wasn't feeling very brave. I felt like I was risking everything, my entire body, my entire life, my entire future, hanging by a single rope tied around my waist and a few sparse tools. I could feel the harness cutting into my skin, but it didn't matter if it was uncomfortable. I hollered into my walkie-talkie. Everything's good, Zack.

That's good, Father. OK. Holler if you need me! Roger, I reply. I tried to put my walkie-talkie back into my pocket, but my gloved hand let it slip and my walkie-talkie dropped. I can still see it slowly gyrating in the sky as it made its twenty-five-foot descent to clatter and splatter on the rocks below.

There is only one way out, and that was to ascend, even with risk. I find that is what life is like as a Christian. Theirs is always one way ahead, and that's forward. So that's what I did! Stroke after stroke, wedging my four-foot placement, there were times I felt breathless from the strenuous climb. I could feel the rope tug.

The sun was setting late on that late afternoon and the shadow of the canyon froze even more as the temperatures began to drop. At this point, no one was climbing next below or next to me. I could hear the clattering voices of the young people, but they couldn't see or her me. I thought to myself, that maybe they were sitting somewhere playing cards, praying the rosary, and laughing as their priest was hanging, and in deathless defiance of gravity over the edge of what felt like certain death.

At times like these, you don't think about what you'd have to lose. You can only think of what you need to do to move forward. Before the water froze, it descended like a waterfall. There were several uneven spots I had to navigate.

My arms were aching, my head was throbbing, and sweat was dripping into my eyes. I didn't have a walkie-talkie to communicate my fears. There are times you think that you're alone, obstacles come, awareness of risks arise, then you remember... Jesus is calling you there. And if he's calling you, there, he'll see you through.

Immense waves of gratitude for God's presence, flooded my heart. He entrusted me with risks before, and saw me through them. I picked my way over the ledge, forcing my way beyond exhaustion to the top of that icy cliff.

I remember many things from that climb. But I remember even more, the blessing that came from realizing that Jesus was climbing with me, whether It was on that mountain or through my ministry. Every step and every risk I would take in my ministry. He called me to bravely follow Him.

REFLECTION

PAUSE:

Spend a few minutes in silence, settling into a comfortable place where you can allow your body to relax. If there are a few areas that you are still tight or tense, notice that and take a couple deep breaths to release the tension and offer it to God.

PONDER:

- After reading the story, what struck you the most?
- Were there some themes you resonated with?
- Themes that you noticed a resistance within you?
- I invite you to read Isaiah 41: 4-10

"I, the Lord, the first, and with the last am He. The coastlands have seen, and are afraid, the ends of the earth tremble; they have drawn near and come. Everyone helps his neighbor, one says to his brother, "Take courage!" The craftsman encourages the goldsmith, and he who smooths with the hammer, who strikes the anvil, saying of the soldering, "It is good!" and they fasten it with nails so that it cannot be moved. But you, Israel, my servant, Jacob, whom I have chosen, offspring of Abraham, my friend; you whom I took from the ends of the earth, and called from its farthest corners, saying to you, You are my servant, I have chosen you, and not cast you off; Fear not, for I am with you, be not dismayed, for I am your God; I will strengthen you, I will help you, I will uphold you with my victorious right hand."

What word or phrase stood out for you?

PRAY:

Talk with God about it; then, ask God what he would like to say to you about it?

PRACTICE:

Together with God, consider one concrete action step you can take today based on what you heard, read, or experienced during this time.

CLOSING PRAYER (OPTIONAL OR YOUR OWN):

Dear Lord,
Teach me how to trust in your ways, to take risks, and fulfill your purposes in my life. Sometimes, you stretch me to step out far beyond my comfort zone, not to test me, but to strengthen and mature me. May I become more deeply aware of where you lead and have the courage to follow, so I may lead others to you too. In Jesus' Name, Amen.
*Father Nathan Cromly, CSJ: Western Colorado

JOURNAL ENTRY

Desert Trek*

∞

"give me an undivided heart"
Psalm 86:11 (NRSVCE)

Have you ever had a yearning to just "get away" from life? To go somewhere different? To shift your thinking while taking time reflecting, savoring pivotal times of growth, relaxing, considering the future?

Later in 2019, I pondered how I could mark the significant milestone of turning 50 in early April of 2020. As I prayed, a deep desire to spend some time in the desert grew. I imagined walking beside the Lord in the desert, like two best friends journeying together. I kept hearing the words, "Come away with Me, let's walk for a while."

Marking the beginning of this new, monumental year, in January 2020, my prayer became a reality! I headed to a simple hermitage in Albuquerque, New Mexico, eagerly anticipating this time away. Situated on 75 acres in the high desert, with the backdrop of the Sandia Mountains, sunrises were brilliant, and sunsets reflected a breathtaking, watermelon colored hue. During the day, I spent time walking, often barefoot, sandy trails...grounding my thinking and conversing with God. A short walk from my hermitage was a desert chapel. Inside, were cushioned benches, a stone semi-circular fireplace, thoughtfully appointed icons, and Jesus, present in the tabernacle. I loved spending time here. It was here that it seemed He spoke the loudest, inviting me to reflect on the same question over and over... "Where is your heart, child...where is your heart?"

My head told me how I "should" answer, but as the week went on, I became increasingly aware that my heart didn't follow. With this honest revelation, I became disoriented and unsettled. I wondered how I had been so subtly dis-connected through rationalizing some of the not so healthy choices I had made in my life. God created the sacred, gentle space to meet him here, without any harsh criticism, yet like a loving parent, gently and firmly challenging me to further growth.

Toward the end of the week, the answer gradually became clear. It was time to have an undivided heart...for Him! I had to shed any self-made, egoistic, mini-gods in my life. My identity had been so wrapped up in my work, ministry, and the affirmation of others. It's not that these gifts weren't good, I just allowed myself to elevate them above Him! Wow, how subtly these "good" gifts became "better" gifts than God! This revelation was humbling and painful, yet the Lord gently, firmly, and lovingly led me out of this proverbial experience of darkness. The light of freedom and levity, a reorientation of my choices and desires, gradually began to restoring with His help. This would be a good year ahead...a year to live my most authentic self, to whom God had always intended for me to be.

REFLECTION

PAUSE:

Spend a few minutes in silence, settling into a comfortable place where you can allow your body to relax. If there are a few areas that you are still tight or tense, notice that and take a couple deep breaths to release the tension and offer it to God.

PONDER:

- After reading the story, what struck you the most?
- Were there some themes you resonated with?
- Themes that you noticed a resistance within you?
- I invite you to read Psalm 86:11

"Teach me your way, Lord, that I may walk in your truth; give me an undivided heart, to revere your name."

What word or phrase stood out for you?

PRAY:

Talk with God about it; then, ask God what he would like to say to you about it?

PRACTICE:

Together with God, consider one concrete action step you can take today based on what you heard, read, or experienced during this time.

CLOSING PRAYER (OPTIONAL OR YOUR OWN):

Dear Lord,
Thank you for always patiently pursuing us, walking with us, and sharing your gentle, firm, and loving guidance as we grow with You. Give us the grace to accept our imperfect humanity, imperfect love, yet to hear Your firm Truth with gentle invitations to reorient our hearts towards You above all else. May we bear fruit, through Your Divine Design, in all of our relationships, including with ourselves. We pray for all these things in all of our todays and tomorrows. In Jesus' name. Amen.

*Heather Makowicz: Santa Maria De La Vid Abbey, Albuquerque, New Mexico

JOURNAL ENTRY

ENTRY # 21

PADDLE BOARDING*

"For everything, there is a season..."
Ecclesiastes 3:1–4 (NRSVCE)

There are many things vying for our attention. Relationships, occupation, dreams, goals, the media, the culture, and oh yes, the most important aspect of our lives, having a close relationship with God!

About eight years ago, I went paddle boarding for the first time with a friend in Cape May, New Jersey. We were excited to try an eco-tour, and to experience the wildness of nature while challenging ourselves to something new. I was particularly fascinated by the idea of being as close to "walking on water" as you could get in this lifetime!

When it was time, we headed out into the warm, slow moving, bay water. One thing the outfitter guide forgot to mention...it was jellyfish season! I thought to myself, "I better nail this, or I'm dumping and getting stung!" Surprisingly, I glided into the water smoothly. Whew! My friend, on the other hand, stepped onto the board, and immediately rolled right into the water surrounded by jellyfish! Yikes! With an adolescent-like chuckle, I unsympathetically blurted out, "I'm glad it wasn't me!" After a good, shared belly laugh, we recovered joyfully taking in the feast of the senses, paddling, listening to the birds chirping, watching fish swim right under our boards, and feeling the warm sun's rays against our skin.

Since this was our first time, initially, we were very conscious of how to shift our weight, adjusting periodically to maintain equilibrium in the center of the board. As we continued along, we began to intuitively sense how to move our body to steer the boards and keep afloat.

Like staying afloat on a paddle board, our lives need balance to stay healthy. Prioritizing our day can be a challenge! When we allow God to be our Guide, He leads us in our experiences. After a while, we begin to notice when we are off balance and need to shift our weight to what is most important. He reveals to us His priorities for the day, and slowly transforms our dogged efforts to trusting His plan to unfold.

How can we live, love, and serve, with patience and trust that God has a divinely appointed plan for all of us? Grounding this concept in everyday life, how I might apply this to my life right now. Depending on the day, this prayer can feel daunting and impossible, or flexible and freeing.

Have you ever sensed the pressing need for balance in your life? If so, do you wonder if this word "balance" is even possible?

REFLECTIONS:

PAUSE:

Spend a few minutes in silence and settle into a comfortable place where you can allow your body to relax. If there are a few areas that you are still tight or tense, notice that and take a couple deep breaths to release the tension and offer it to God.

PONDER:

- After reading the story, what struck you the most?
- Were there some themes you resonated with?
- What themes did you notice a resistance within you?
- I invite you to read Ecclesiastes 3:1-4

"For everything there is a season, and a time for every matter under heaven; a time to be born, and a time to die; a time to plant, and a time to pluck up what is planted; a time to kill, and a time to heal; a time to break down, and a time to build up; a time to weep, and a time to laugh; a time to mourn, and a time to dance"

What word or phrase stood out for you?

PRAY:

Talk to God and ask him what he would like to say to you about it?

PRACTICE:

Together with God, consider one concrete action step you can take today based on what you heard, read, or experienced during this time.

CLOSING PRAYER (OPTIONAL OR YOUR OWN):

Dear Lord,
You know every detail of my life. You have placed me in this time, this place, with these relationships, and in these circumstances. Help me to remember that you are the Divine

Orchestrator, who conducts our life with reason, purpose, and time. With the help of Your Holy Spirit, I ask you to bring balance to those areas in our lives that need tending and help us to release what is not ours to carry, at least for today. Help me with your guidance and discernment to lead me to what most needs my attention today, and to ask for the grace to be at peace with unfinished business. Show me how to keep in perspective the balance of the connecting with You through prayer, study, and living/working in daily life. I am reminded that You are ordinary as well as extraordinary! In Jesus' Name, Amen.

*Heather Makowicz: Marsh Creek State Park, Downingtown, Pennsylvania

JOURNAL ENTRY

ENTRY # 22

STEMMING*

∞

"Trust in the Lord with all your heart and
do not lean on your own understanding."
Proverbs 3:5 (NIV)

I n Utah, the dry heat was bearable since humidity was non-existent. But it was still an intense 101-degree day.

A few of us went to the Tuacahn Saddle, a strenuous hike through the Red Cliffs Desert Reserve and into Snow Canyon. After a long day's effort, we were rewarded at the pinnacle with an incredible view of the canyon. It's multifaceted topography of sand, sandstone, jagged rocks, with bright blue skies as a backdrop. We earned the rest and the magnificent view.

The hike required us to be deeply attentive to our footing and to use various technical climbing methods to get to the top. One of these climbs required us to use a scary, yet thrilling, new-to-me method called, "stemming." In order to keep from falling or slipping, you have to press your feet firmly into the sandstone, spreading your legs with each side using equal and opposite force against each side wall.

At first, it felt awkward, uncomfortable, and I struggled to get my bearings. But as I continued from one deep crevice to the next, it became much easier. Before long, this new way of climbing renewed my confidence in different techniques. I felt like a modern Spiderman!

With stemming, I need to hold my body upright while evenly distributing my weight between two vertical rocks. I remembered this experience later when I struggled for clarity around an important issue. I'd wrestled with it in prayer for a time and had decided to bring it to a few wise friends. I scheduled a meeting to share my honest thoughts, and to be quite frank, I was anxious.

My go-to interior pattern was to "people please" and to have "peace at all costs." I believed that if I expressed strong disagreement, even if in a firm and calm manner, others might judge me as being wrong, confused, or just plain incompetent. I struggled with giving myself the permission to disagree with a situation when I had a deep conviction.

When I applied the lessons of stemming to this situation, I found myself asking the Lord how I might figuratively "hold the tension" in this situation without either abandoning myself through people pleasing or going in with my ego, holding a non-verbal, self-righteous attitude.

After about a week of pondering and praying, the Lord reminded me about how he held the tension between two situations, that is, experiencing fully his humanity, while entering fully into his Divinity. If he experienced such a delicate balancing act, why wouldn't we be asked to do the same?

I realized that holding the tension in the midst of two sides of a situation, is actually where we too, are invited to be. I am not called to insulate, to isolate, or to avoid, but to be where I am, to have those difficult, uncomfortable dialogues with people who have different perspectives, and to sometimes sit in the awkwardness. After all, how do we grow, unless we allow ourselves to come close to one another, broken and beautiful all at the same time?

As a spiritual director, I was presented with thought provoking questions. One of our professors would gently challenge us with this evocative suggestion, perhaps this is your "growing edge". If we want to experience life fully, we need to become comfortable with the uncomfortable, to "stem" between the circumstances and the people in our lives that aren't necessarily easy to bear and be open to the invitation of transformation there.

REFLECTION

PAUSE:

Spend a few minutes in silence and settle into a comfortable place where you can allow your body to relax. If there are a few areas that you are still tight or tense, notice that and take a couple deep breaths to release the tension and offer it to God.

PONDER:

- After reading the story, what struck you the most?
- Were there some themes you resonated with?
- What themes did you notice a resistance within you?
- I invite you to read Isaiah 43:18-19

"Forget the former things; do not dwell in the past. See, I am doing a new thing! Now, it springs up; do you not perceive it? I am making a way in the wilderness and streams in the wasteland."

What word or phrase stood out for you?

PRAY:

Talk to God and ask him what he would like to say to you about it?

PRACTICE:

Together with God, consider one concrete action step you can take today based on what you heard, read, or experienced during this time.

CLOSING PRAYER (OPTIONAL OR YOUR OWN):

Dear Lord,
Thank you for your examples of how you "stemmed" between two extremes. You laid down the path for us to follow but did not force us to move in that direction. You were generous with your love, even when everyone around you was limited with

theirs. You always call us back unconditionally to yourself, even when we struggle to love.

Please give us the grace to step out boldly, lovingly, and humbly, with individuals with whom we may not see eye-to-eye. We ask for your gentle challenge to love like you in the midst of our own imperfect love and to believe that is enough. Please give us the grace to lean into the ways you would have us understand a situation, rather than our own comprehension. In Jesus' Name, Amen.

*Heather Makowicz: Tuacahn Saddle (Padre Canyon), St. George, Utah

~ *Stemming** ~

JOURNAL ENTRY

FISHING*

∞

"I have said these things to you, that in me you may have peace.
In the world, you will have tribulation. But take heart;
I have overcome the world." John 16:33

We began fishing together while we were dating. It was then, and continues to be, an easy way to experience nature, have deep conversation, and reminisce about childhood memories whether on a boat, on the shore, or standing knee-deep in the wake. As life has gotten more complicated, we yearn for days that we can grab our tackle box and rods and head to the water.

Both of us love animals- all living creatures in fact. One of us is a fish eater, while the other can't stand the site of scales and gills near a plate. For that reason, we practice the "catch and release" method. It's a slightly more challenging way to fish as the hooks lack barbs, but when the bait is good, and the fish plentiful, even we can find success. Taking additional methods to protect the fish, we wear gloves, and monitor their time out of the water. We are grateful for the opportunity to see God's creation up close and enjoy watching our frightened friends swim happily back to their home.

Recently we sought isolation in Northwestern Pennsylvania at one of our favorite state parks. While we take many fishing and camping trips throughout the year, we return to this spot every year. We were both struggling with all that the world was throwing our way. Though the stresses of our lives often build slowly over time, one day in our fishing hole brings so much relief.

Once we settled in, we rented a pontoon boat and trekked to a remote part of the large man-made lake. We anchored in a small cove where we could see the shore, the lake, and the nearby hillside. Gently rocking with the ripples, we cast our lines and enjoy the pause. In that moment, our senses are awakened. Hearing the beautiful sounds of nature, smelling the fresh, clean air, and seeing all the colors in God's palate, we felt safe, loved, and cared for by the one who created everything around us.

We spent many hours on the water, occasionally reeling in a small bluegill, or sunfish, even a long pike, working together, to ensure their safe return to their habitat. I doubt the creatures enjoy the ride from the water to the boat, but they are quickly reunited with their fellow lake dwellers.

For us, there's an excitement in the catch. We frequently hold mini competitions, who can lure the first fish, the biggest fish, and the most fish. As much as we love the sporting aspect of reeling in the temporary prize, there is an equal sense of joy in the release. We know that we're sending them back into the loving protection of Him, their creator. Whether minnows or bass, bottom feeders, or trout, they are part of something so much bigger. As are we.

And as we bring our boat back to shore, we reflect on the goodness of the day. Knowing that God is there, in the silence. He's there in the yearning for peace. God is quietly protecting all the life, seen and unseen, naming all the creatures. Most of all, He is with us, even when we don't see Him, protecting us, moving in us, loving us.

REFLECTION

PAUSE:

Spend a few minutes in silence, settling into a comfortable place where you can allow your body to relax. If there are a few areas that you are still tight or tense, notice that and take a couple deep breaths to release the tension and offer it to God.

PONDER:

- After reading the story, what struck you the most?
- Were there some themes you resonated with?
- Themes that you noticed a resistance within you?
- I invite you to read John 16:33

"I have said these things to you, that in me you may have peace. In the world, you will have tribulation. But take heart; I have overcome the world."

What word or phrase stood out for you?

PRAY:

Talk with God about it; then, ask God what he would like to say to you about it?

PRACTICE:

Together with God, consider one concrete action step you can take today based on what you heard, read, or experienced during this time.

CLOSING PRAYER (OPTIONAL OR YOUR OWN):

Dear Lord,
Thank you for gifting all of creation, whether plant, animal, and most of all, all of humanity with life. Thank you for the water, wildlife, the woods, and all of natural creation you have offered us as a portal of entry to encounter You. When silence is given to me in those sacred spaces, help me to be aware of your

desire to connect with me and protect me from the whiles of this unhealed world. Reveal to me Your invitation in how I can bring Your Holy Spirit received in those moments back to my workplace, home, and my busy, daily life. In Jesus Name, Amen!
*Lori Blake Tedjeske: Northwestern Pennsylvania

JOURNAL ENTRY

_____

_____

_____

_____

_____

_____

_____

_____

_____

_____

_____

_____

_____

_____

_____

_____

_____

_____

Entry # 24

Photography*

∞

"For in him were created all things in heaven and on earth."
Colossians 1:16 (NKJV)

I don't consider myself a photographer. I never took a class, and I don't own an expensive camera. That said, there is something deep within me that yearns to capture the beauty of creation.

My love of photography grew when my family and I moved to Switzerland. Living in one of the most beautiful countries in the world certainly helped. Whether it was the majestic Swiss Alps, the turquoise color of the pristine lakes, or the rugged landscapes surrounding the thousands of hiking trails, Switzerland's beauty engulfed us. There were unlimited amounts of beauty to capture, resulting in an infinite desire to want more pictures.

The Swiss theologian, Hans Urs von Balthasar, believed that you could find God by starting with the beautiful. In essence, when beauty strikes us, we will want to then participate in it. For example, we want to live in beautiful places; we want to visit beautiful cathedrals and listen to beautiful music. Once we begin to participate, we find the good. Finally, both the beauty and the good lead us to the truth. My pastor refers to seeing the whole truth as a journey to find the truth about ourselves, others, life, and God. This journey certainly takes time and happens throughout our lives. My journey has included a camera.

Switzerland's natural beauty arrested me. It gave me energy and tapped into a yearning that I knew oh so well. It was the same yearning that I feel in the presence of the Eucharist. A longing for communion with God. Consequently, I began to take my camera everywhere. I couldn't get enough of the beauty that surrounded me. As a result, it didn't take long for that beauty to invite me to participate more fully. I hiked. I skied. I sat on a bench for hours, just looking. I took boat rides and train rides for the sole purpose to marvel at the beautiful landscapes. I would stop the car on my way to the grocery store to snap a picture of a single tree. Everywhere I went, I had a camera ready to capture the moment—capture the beauty.

Every click of the camera button was a prayer. It was an attempt to fulfill the deep desires within me. A desire to love and be loved. A desire to know and be known. As I participated more fully, I began to understand the movement and ways of how God could speak to me through His creation. I began to understand His truth through nature. In front of our house, the small creek, which quietly verbalized great mercy, was one example of this revelation.

We lived in Worb, Switzerland. It was a small village outside of Bern. Our house sat on a hill and was surrounded by rolling hills with the Alps' views from the back. It was breathtaking. And yet, there, quietly, and mundanely, the small creek's water flowed, unnoticeable to many who walked by its path due to the grandeur of the mountains.

My boys liked to ride their bikes alongside it. I would stroll and listen to the gentle water moving ever so steadily. The consistent cadence of the water was peaceful, while its never-ending flow was bountiful. I would stop and shut my eyes. During these moments, the small unnoticeable creek brought me to times when I experienced our Lord's great mercy. During my darkest times, the moments of feeling unloved and unworthy, there alongside me stood Jesus. The moments right after leaving the confessional. That small creek was a reminder of the cleansing water that would gush from the Lord's side on Calvary.

The creek was the object of my desires that would result in hundreds of photographs because it reflected the beauty, the good, and the truth of God's mercy.

It has been a year since we have moved back to the United States. I still don't consider myself a photographer. That said, I think of myself as someone who prays with a camera. I guess I am a grateful man who yearns to capture God's infinite love and beauty with every photo while sending prayers with every touch of the button.

REFLECTION

PAUSE:

Spend a few minutes in silence, settling into a comfortable place where you can allow your body to relax. If there are a few areas that you are still tight or tense, notice that and take a couple deep breaths to release the tension and offer it to God.

PONDER:

- After reading the story, what struck you the most?
- Were there some themes you resonated with?
- Themes that you noticed a resistance within you?
- I invite you to read Colossians 1:16

"For in him were created all things that are in heaven and on earth, visible and invisible, whether thrones or dominions or principalities or powers. All things were created through Him and for Him."

What word or phrase stood out for you?

PRAY:

Talk with God about it; then, ask God what he would like to say to you about it?

PRACTICE:

Together with God, consider one concrete action step you can take today based on what you heard, read, or experienced during this time.

CLOSING PRAYER (OPTIONAL OR YOUR OWN):

Lord, My God, I thank you for your wondrous creation. I thank you for your beauty, which dazzles me. I thank you for your goodness, visible in your created beauty.
I thank you for the truth…that you are Love, and for offering me a place alongside all of creation to worship your goodness. Amen.
*Brett Illig: Worb, Switzerland

JOURNAL ENTRY

_____

_____

_____

_____

_____

_____

_____

_____

_____

_____

_____

_____

_____

_____

_____

_____

_____

_____

_____

_____

WATCHING BIRDS*

∞

"But ask the animals, and they will teach you."
Job 12:7 (NIV)

The Jesuit priest Walter Ciszek spent twenty-three difficult years in the Soviet Union, fifteen of them in Soviet prisons or so-called "working camps" in Siberia. He wrote a great book about his experience, *With God in Russia*. I have read it several times because it is a fascinating life story and wonderfully written. He lived in different prisons, in environments where he experienced a lot of violence, fighting, killing, stealing, hate, and where people were often seen as mere numbers and treated with no dignity. Ciszek (who in Russia used the name Vladimir) experienced many beatings and several times he almost lost his life. Once, there was a huge fight between the prisoners and the soldiers guarding them in Camp 5. Many prisoners were brutally killed. There is an exceptional chapter where Ciszek reflects on this event. When I read it for the first time, I was surprised how much attention he pays describing an experience with a bird family. Here is a part of that chapter:

From Camp 5 we were led off straight into the tundra. The soldiers seemed so nervous and tense, I thought for sure we were to be shot. I began to pray. We walked about 5 miles to the west. It was almost 5 a.m. when we came to a grassy area, marshy and wet and dotted with thick shrubbery … I was so hungry I tried to eat handfuls of grass when the guards weren't looking.

We were brought in to work the quarry. We had to live in it too. Guards were stationed around the top of the quarry, and we were told that if anyo*ne tried to leave the pits he would be shot on sight. We were assigned to work, two by two, and given a specific number of carloads of stone to be quarried, loaded into small hand cars, and towed to the crusher every day. It was impossible to fulfill the quota, set deliberately high, even in twelve hours of work, and it was like working in the antechambers of hell… ——*

I began to think about Camp 5 and the men who had died there, those who had confessed and those who hadn't. Then I thought of home, of my sisters and friends who had no idea where I was, and I wondered what they were doing; of my early days in school, of the time when I first served Mass – a real sentimental jag! I tried to snap myself out of it; I was beginning to get so emotionally worked up that my body was trembling. I was afraid I might have a breakdown.

I looked down from the top of the hopper and saw a bird with a nest of two young ones on a grassy hillock just across the railroad tracks. The mother was feeding them, flying off and returning, while the father stayed there and held them in the nest. I became fascinated and lost my train of thought. I even forgot how tired I was, and felt a sudden surge of joy. Then, somehow, I remembered my father feeding me in the small hours of the morning when I had returned penniless, tired, and scared from a Boy Scout outing. From that thought, my mind wandered again to the men who had been killed in Camp 5, and I thought how their mothers and fathers had protected them in childhood.

I could feel the tears welling up in my eyes. I was almost ready to break down completely when I felt a slap on the back! It was another prisoner who had come looking for me. "Vladimir," he said, "go get your supper. I put it away for you." "Look down there," I said and began to point out to him how the father and mother bird were taking care of the little ones. (Ciszek, pp. 254-257)

I believe watching that bird family, Ciszek was touched by their care, love, freedom – something he himself was missing and longing for. He did not know that, at that very time, there were many people praying, caring, trying to set him free, and get him back home. But at that moment, it was seeing the birds that brought him peace and calmed him down. "I even forgot how tired I was, and felt a sudden surge of joy" (Ciszek, pp.254-257). The birds reminded him of the care his father gave him when he was young. Then, his heart was over-whelmed with compassion toward the killed prisoners, as he thought about their mothers and fathers protecting them in childhood. To me, this is an example of a "sensitive contemplative heart." Ciszek was able to see where the Grace of God is present or absent. At this moment, he was able to gaze with love at this sign of the caring birds and to see God there. Are not joy and peace fruits of the Holy Spirit? Yes, this was a moment of Grace.

I reflected on this story again, after I got Covid 19. I contracted the infection while serving as a chaplain to the sick people at Mercy Fitzgerald Hospital near Philadelphia. I spent forty days and forty nights in isolation.

The first week of this time I felt bad, anxious, not knowing what to expect from this illness. The anxiety and the isolation were not at all pleasant. At the Abbey where I lived, while I could not leave my room, I was able to open my window to watch the birds outside. There was a wonderful old tree right under my window and different kinds of birds liked to rest there. One day there was a couple of Mourning Doves. Their "dance of love" was beautiful. They slowly approached each other, they gently touched and "kissed." Their tenderness deeply touched my soul. It was a moment of grace. I took a few pictures and then I enjoyed this moment, praying and resting in the realization of God's loving compassion for me. Like Ciszek, birds became messengers of God's love for me.

REFLECTION

PAUSE:

Spend a few minutes in silence, settling into a comfortable place where you can allow your body to relax. If there are a few areas that you are still tight or tense, notice that and take a couple deep breaths to release the tension and offer it to God.

PONDER:

- After reading the story, what struck you the most?
- Were there some themes you resonated with?
- Themes that you noticed a resistance within you?
- I invite you to read Job 12:7–10

"But ask the animals, and they will teach you, or the birds of the sky, and they will tell you; or speak to the earth, and it will teach you, or let the fish in the sea inform you. Which of all these does not know that the hand of the Lord has done this? In his hand is the life of every creature and the breath of all mankind."

What word or phrase stood out for you?

PRAY:

Talk with God about it; then, ask God what he would like to say to you about it? Practice:

Together with God, consider one concrete action step you can take today based on what you heard, read, or experienced during this time.

CLOSING PRAYER (OPTIONAL OR YOUR OWN):

Dear Lord,
Thank you for all of your living creatures, both big and small.
Sometimes I can move through my day so fast that I forget to
stop and savor the little gifts right in front of me, like a bird, a

chipmunk, and a butterfly. Help me to listen and to more deeply experience these messengers of hope, healing, and joy right in my very own backyard. Thank you! In Jesus' Name, Amen!
*Mirslov Jordanek, OPraem : Daylesford Abbey, Paoli, Pennsylvania

JOURNAL ENTRY

Sunset*

∞

Limitless Power

"He heals the brokenhearted and binds up their wounds. He determines the number of stars; gives to all of them their names."
Psalm 147: 3-4 (ESV)

"Said the rain to the wind, 'you push and I'll pelt.'
They so smote the garden bed that the flowers actually knelt,
And lay low but not dead. I know how the flowers felt.
– Robert Frost

I sat on the lifeguard chair as the sun set over the ocean. My world turned upside down and the emotions I felt were as overwhelming as the waves crashing into the shore.

Two weeks earlier I gave birth to a beautiful baby girl. Five days earlier I signed adoption papers that relinquished my rights as her mother and saw her for the last time at the agency. I knew at the time of the signing and during the months leading up to her birth that I was making the right decision for her. I had prayed about, planned, and prepared for that moment. I knew it was going to be the hardest thing I'd ever done. But the knowledge didn't prepare me for the first of many waves of raw emotion.

Some family members brought me to the beach for a few days for a change of scenery and to rest and recover. The ocean had always been a place of restoration for me. That evening I took a walk on the beach. I could feel strong things stirring in my heart and I knew I wanted to be alone when they broke the surface. The cold sand and sea air felt good and I climbed the empty lifeguard chair to watch the sun slowly disappear on the other side of the ocean. It wasn't a dramatic sunset, throwing stunning hues of orange, pink, and purple across the sky. It was quiet and clear with muted blues and wisps of white and a hint of orange dotting the horizon. It's light trailed upon the water, glistening and swaying with the swells of the water. And there, it's simple beauty pierced my heart and everything that I had been feeling and carrying was undone and came crashing over me, wave after wave. Tears flowed in an endless stream as I rocked and wrapped my arms around myself, physically trying to hold my broken heart together.

Feeling lost and alone in that grief and pain, I tried recounting all the right reasons why I made the decision for adoption. And even though they were still right, they were as lost as I was in the vastness of grief like drops of water in the churning ocean that stretched out before me.

I felt small and helpless, like a child, pleading with God for something, anything, and screaming into the sea until I couldn't scream anymore. Falling back into the chair, empty and exhausted, I looked at that quiet sun setting over the ocean and I knew God was there. He invited me into His presence. I knew in that instant He saw me, that He heard me, and that He was present to my pain. I felt no shame—just love and acceptance. I can't explain exactly how I knew but I knew that I knew. It was as if the glory of His presence stretched out before me in the clear light of the sunset. It's warmth was intensifying even as it was setting and I felt His peace bathe me in warmth. And as the warm tears started to flow down my cheeks again, I felt His gentle kiss in the ocean breeze that touched my face. And in the power of the ocean that minutes earlier had seemed cold and angry, I felt the strength and protection of a God who loves me fiercely and deeply, a God who would not let any harm come to me. I was overcome by His love as He roared in the waves and whispered in the wind, again and again, "I am here. You are not alone. I've got you. And I knew then that everything was going to be okay. I knew that I would not feel crushed forever. And I knew that I had made the right decision because the God who showed up for me in that moment was the same God who would watch over my birth daughter with that same fierce and protective love.

REFLECTIONS

PAUSE:

Spend a few minutes in silence, settling into a comfortable place where you can allow your body to relax. If there are a few areas that you are still tight or tense, notice that and take a couple deep breaths to release the tension and offer it to God.

PONDER:

*After reading the story, what struck you the most?
*Were there some themes you resonated with?
*Themes that you noticed a resistance within you?
*I invite you to read Psalm 147: 3-4

"He heals the brokenhearted and binds up their wounds. He determines the number of stars; gives to all of them their names."

What word or phrase stood out for you?

PRAY:

Talk with God about it; then, ask God what he would like to say to you about it?

PRACTICE:

Together with God, consider one concrete action step you can take today based on what you heard, read, or experienced during this time.

CLOSING PRAYER (OPTIONAL OR YOUR OWN):

Dear Lord,
I know that you are a good and merciful God. You never leave or abandon me. But sometimes, when you are inviting me into loving like you, my heart is stretched to breaking and the pain feels unbearable. I feel alone and helpless. Help me, in those moments, to trust and surrender my pain to your purifying love, so that may become an open vessel of your love. In Jesus Name, Amen
*Jeannine: Cape Cod, Massachusetts

Journal Entry

WATERFALL PLUNGE*

∞

"Then he said to me, "Prophesy to these bones"
Ezekiel 37:4-5 (NRSVCE)

Dave and I went to Puerto Rico during one of his Navy assignments. Being nature and adventure lovers, we had to find a rainforest! We found La Mina Waterfall, in El Yunque National Forest, in Puerto Rico, where you could swim! I was excited, yet fearful since the waterfall seemed so powerful. At times, when I swam underneath it, I was afraid the force of the waterfall would push me under! Pressing past my fear, I swam to the backside. When I did, I experienced the immense beauty of this God-created waterfall from a rare view.

Fast forward to present time. We had a meeting with the directors regarding our twenty-one-year-old-son, Nate. He would age out of supportive services through the Department of Education at the end of the school year. We desired to create the highest level of supportive independence for him and the consolidated waiver was nearly impossible to receive. The dreaded news came, nothing available. This was discouraging, to say the least!

I know discouragement can be one of the enemy's greatest tactics to separate us from God. I asked friends and family to join us in prayer for a breakthrough!

A week went by, and I headed to Encounter Ministries School of Prophecy. Prophecy is a charismatic gift, given to us by the Holy Spirit. It is a way the Holy Spirit can divinely accelerate our faith to those open to receiving it, reminding us that our future is in God's hands.

On the last night, we broke out into prophetic teams to give and receive words. When it was my turn, a person shared an image. In this image, our family was together with Nate in the middle. In front of our family was a fortified dam. Behind the dam were legions of angels stacked up, eager to pour grace onto our family, but something was stopping them. He had a sense that the Lord wanted me to punch through the dam. With all my might, and tears flowing, I punched several times in front of me, pleading for a breakthrough.

Four days later, one of those directors called me and said..." you are NOT GOING TO BELIEVE THIS, but the state announced that Nate's name came up for the consolidated waiver!"

The case workers were in utter shock, initially I was too, wondering if this was for real. I received this confirmation and immediately dropped to my knees thanking Jesus for this breakthrough! The dam broke, and the waters of grace were released. As the directors continued to be astonished by this extremely rare circumstance. A miracle story... the gift of graces poured out like a waterfall!

Like the beauty on the other side of the water wall, grace appeared on the other side of the dam. Sometimes we are asked to walk BOLDLY in faith, to punch through a proverbial dam in prayer with courage and ask for a breakthrough!

REFLECTIONS:

PAUSE:

Spend a few minutes in silence and settle into a comfortable place where you can allow your body to relax. If there are a few areas that you are still tight or tense, notice that and take a couple deep breaths to release the tension and offer it to God.

PONDER:

- After reading the story, what struck you the most?
- Were there some themes you resonated with?
- What themes did you notice a resistance within you?
- I invite you to read Ezekiel 37:4-5

"Then he said to me, "Prophecy to the bones, and say to them: O dry bones, hear the word of the Lord. Thus, says the Lord God to these bones: I will cause breath to enter into you, and you shall live."

What word or phrase stood out for you?

PRAY:

Talk to God and ask him what he would like to say to you about it?

PRACTICE:

Together with God, consider one concrete action step you can take today based on what you heard, read, or experienced during this time.

CLOSING PRAYER (OPTIONAL OR YOUR OWN):

Dear Lord,
You are the God of the impossible. Thank you for the breakthroughs you have already given us in our lives. May we walk in faith, hope, and in courage, that you care and love us even more than we love ourselves. I allow you to lead me in the destiny you have already prepared before me, believing

in firm confidence, of your providential care. Help me to be humble enough to ask others to pray for us when we need it, remembering in Matthew 18:20, that "when two or three are gathered, there You are in the midst." We praise you and we thank you, Lord!
In Jesus' Name, Amen

*Heather Makowicz: La Mina Waterfall, El Yunque National RainForest, Puerto Rico

JOURNAL ENTRY

Entry # 28

Zip Lining*

∞

"For I know the plans I have for you, declares the Lord, plans to
prosper you and not harm you, plans to give you hope and a future."
Jeremiah 29:11(NIV)

My husband Dave visited Costa Rica, to celebrate our 10ᵗʰ wedding anniversary. As usual, I thought it would be fun to try something adventurous, *what's new*?? Costa Rica was known for some of the most incredible zip-line canopy tours in the world!

After some research, I found an outfitter that touted the longest zip lines in Latin America! At approximately 1500 meters long through the rain forest, we would see God's breath-taking creation from a new lens. This course would include 11 zips, a swinging rope bridge, and a MEGA Tarzan swing at a height of 45 meters (145 feet)!

I suited up, with helmet, harness, carabiner lines, and a brand new, stiff leather glove meant to slow down my "ride" – HA! Eager and energetic, I was ready to head out! It was pouring rain, well, what do we expect, it was in a rainforest!

We raced high above the trees, peering at the deep green foliage below. At lightning speed, I flew down the line, screaming with delight on each zip, eagerly anticipating the next one ahead, even if I didn't know exactly what to expect.

Half way, we climbed to a high platform and were ready to take on the Tarzan swing. The woman before me screamed with what sounded like something out of a horror movie as she jumped. I looked down and saw her swing wildly between two trees and a wide-open sky, with a cliff just beyond our visual field. As she slowed down, the guides caught her and gently lowered her to the ground. It was MY TURN!

What I was thinking when I signed up for this. This is ridiculous! I am going to splatter on the ground! What if the bungee snaps in half?

I reassured myself, "you have made it this far, you did the research, this should be safe, just take the leap!"

Three, two one, and I jumped! I screamed with terror, along with a surge of freedom. Since I didn't have wings, this was the closest thing to flying! What a ride! When I reached the bottom, I wondered what if I had not taken the risk to jump?

I continued to ponder this question as we continued. More zips, and the rain picked up. The zips towards the end had sharp declines, making it harder to stop at the platforms. The guides had to catch us before it seemed like we would slam into the tree ahead. Apparently, at this point, I earned a new nickname! I became known as "muy rapido mama".

When we completed our adventure, I asked why I had that nickname? In broken English, the guide snickered and looked at my glove and said, "it means very fast mama!" As we laughed, they disclosed to me that they couldn't believe that I wasn't more scared. They continued to tell me that the glove I wore was brand new, and with new gloves, they take a while to "break in". Apparently, my grip had been pretty loose, allowing me to coast at a crazy speed.

I quipped back, "Great! I was heading towards being the next casualty to make local paper! Laughing, he said, "You're brave! You made it!!"

I couldn't anticipate how the adventure would turn out, even with prudent preparation, I would be safe.

How many times in our faith journey do we question where God is leading? Do we trust Him, even if we can't see what lies in front of us? In this excursion, I had to trust the outfitter, the zip lines, the cables, the carabiner, and the glove. In our journey with Jesus Christ, do we keep our eyes steady on Him and the experiences in our past where we have made it to the other side with Divine assistance?

REFLECTION

PAUSE:

Spend a few minutes in silence, settling into a comfortable place where you can allow your body to relax. If there are a few areas that you are still tight or tense, notice that and take a couple deep breaths to release the tension and offer it to God.

PONDER:

- After reading the story, what struck you the most?
- Were there some themes you resonated with?
- Themes that you noticed a resistance within you?
- I invite you to read Jeremiah 29:11

"For I know the plans I have for you, declares the Lord, plans to prosper you and not harm you, plans to give you hope and a future."

What word or phrase stood out for you?

PRAY:

Talk with God about it; then, ask God what he would like to say to you about it?

PRACTICE:

Together with God, consider one concrete action step you can take today based on what you heard, read, or experienced during this time.

CLOSING PRAYER (OPTIONAL OR YOUR OWN):

Dear Lord, help me remember that you are always with me, even in times that I don't "feel" your presence. Help me to embrace the journey, you have divinely appointed before me, and to have prudence to risk where you have asked for me to go. Thank you for your consistent, faithful, providential love for our lives and may we walk into the future with a steady assurance that you are with us. May the adventures begin! In Jesus' Name, Amen
*Heather Makowicz: Monteverde, Costa Rica

JOURNAL ENTRY

The Bench*

∞

"Come to me, all you who are weary and burdened
and I will give you rest."
Matthew 11:28 (NIV)

I was 10 years into an abusive marriage, working in an overwhelming pressure cooker of a job, struggling with being a stepmom to a beloved teen who had fallen into drugs and alcohol, and a mom to two beautiful young children who I knew were not being raised in a healthy environment. No matter how hard I tried to control everything, fix it all and keep it hidden, I couldn't. It was an incredibly dark and desperate time in my life. I was the epitome of weary and burdened, completely exhausted from trying to find my own solutions.

I began to seek out new ways to engage with him, almost as an experiment to see what would happen. One of the ideas was to attend a silent retreat weekend with my sister Heather. I didn't think I could do it, being an extreme extrovert – all that silence and stillness was really intimidating to me. But it is exactly what is necessary for us to notice Him in our own personal way. At first, I intellectualized how it was all going to go down at the retreat–I had a detailed list of all the prayerful activities I was going to do, in what order, so that God would have the best chance of speaking to me. I had it all mapped out. So I'm walking the labyrinth, reading theological books in the library, journaling on pre-set topics kind of like–see God? I'm giving you the opportunity, go ahead. I'm ready! Annnnd nothing.

It wasn't until I literally laid down, still, and ditched my plan that he did in fact speak to me... profoundly and uniquely. The retreat weekend was drawing to a close, and as I packed, I suddenly *felt* a voice with my whole body. Difficult to describe, but it was like I could hear and fully understand what Jesus was saying instantly and without sound. HIs beautiful message made me stop in my tracks and my heart was beating so fast.

Meet me at the bench I have placed in your heart, meet me there now without haste. I have something there for you.

It was undeniable that Jesus had broken through my barriers of fear and structure, of perceived control and chosen ME, his special and beautiful child. I dropped what I was doing and started walking towards the woods where there was a trail I had not noticed before, did not know existed. I was being guided by a force within me, by him–as if he was holding my hand to show me the way. Deep into the woods we walked until I arrived at a weathered wooden bench in a small clearing surrounded by colorful wildflowers, the sweet smell of honeysuckle and spring grass like a rich perfume, and the sun shining through the trees, bathing everything with golden hues.

I sat on the bench and again felt Jesus' presence, his complex and indescribable essence, sitting next to me. I rested in him and felt more whole than I ever had in my life. As his words seeped into my heart, I took out my notebook and wrote it down so I would always remember meeting my Creator. And what he said to me was this:

Stand in my Light. Lay your head on my mighty, victorious, beautiful chest. Feel my sacred heart beat in synchrony with yours. Feel my left arm around you, stroking your hair, consoling you, protecting you. Be still. Listen to the flowers I am only briefly allowing you to hear me open up for you. Listen to my power and generosity. The flowers pop like tiny snowflakes on ice. The birds are the song of my choirs of angels, worshipping me. The breeze washes over you, through you—cooling and warming at the same time. My world is alive, dancing with life, with freedom, with victory. My heart is consoled with your obedience and friendship. Many do not love me, but I am giving you the love you asked me for in my name—the love you need to love me back. Love wins. Love conquers sin.

Rely on this moment throughout your life. You will not forget it. Not only will I help you to remember, I will add to it as the years pass. I promise to bless you with this memory—our shared moment together, forever.

Feel my arms around you. My head tilted toward yours, nestling your beautiful cheek that I lovingly created. You are my masterpiece. I would have done it all just for you if I had to even if it was only for you—that's how precious you are to me. The agony, the pain, and suffering were all worth it and more to feel your heart intertwined with mine in this moment.

In the Eucharist remember: when you receive my body, I fortify you. Our hearts are joined together. Through my blood I was over you, wash through you, wash away your iniquity and cleanse your sins with my life-giving blood. Sin and death are conquered through me.

I am revealing this to you because you are my friend, my child, my precious treasure. Allow me to stay in your heart always. Keep me right here, as we are now. If you seek me, you will find me. Do not fear my words or actions in any way. For I know the plans I have for you (Jeremiah 29:11)

You will continue to hear my voice. You are on the right track.

A seismic shift happened in my life–I reconciled with someone I considered an enemy for 10 years, went to confession for the first time in 20+ years, and discovered the perfection of Eucharistic Adoration. I experienced the depth and strength of holy friendships. That seed grows into a beautiful flower and that flower is Christ within us.

REFLECTION

PAUSE:

Spend a few minutes in silence, settling into a comfortable place where you can allow your body to relax. If there are a few areas that you are still tight or tense, notice that and take a couple deep breaths to release the tension and offer it to God.

PONDER:

- After reading the story, what struck you the most?
- Were there some themes you resonated with?
- Themes that you noticed a resistance within you?
- I invite you to read, Matthew 11:28

"Come to me, all you who are weary and burdened and I will give you rest."

What word or phrase stood out for you?

PRAY:

Talk with God about it; then, ask God what he would like to say to you about it?

PRACTICE:

Together with God, consider one concrete action step you can take today based on what you heard, read, or experienced during this time.

CLOSING PRAYER (OPTIONAL OR YOUR OWN):

Dear Lord, thank you for showing me your love through creation and teaching me about your attributes. May I always long for you no matter where I go. May I stop and observe your creation and know that You love me.
*Elizabeth Hoisington: Jesuit Retreat House for Spiritual Growth, Wernersville, Pennsylvania, Silent Retreat

JOURNAL ENTRY

SUNRISE*

∞

"His mercies are new every morning."
Lamentations 3:23 (NIV)

The early morning hours are a juxtaposition of sounds: a heavy silence from the sleeping residents and no traffic and a rousing roar of waves. Silent in some ways and yet boisterously powerful.

The sand is always cold in the morning echoing the chill of the ocean night. As my bare feet sink into the smooth coolness, the slightly humid and salty air touches my face and tousles my hair. I feel awake and alive. Sitting at the water's edge, as waves roll in and sneak back out, I marvel at God's perfection and his magnitude.

It is going to happen again. A new day. A new sunrise. A new set of opportunities. A new day of mercies.

Sitting on the beach early in the morning is always by invitation, an internal stirring of longing to see a spectacular feat by a great God. It comes as a sudden thought and sounds intriguing and exciting—sunrise!

How about getting up and watching the sun peek over the ocean and spend some time with me? That is a hard invitation to turn down.

He always shows up. I see him as the first light casts over the sky giving you a glimpse of what is coming. It seems slow in the waiting but then, suddenly, there is the most brilliant crescent of bright blood orange and my heart skips a beat. The crescent turns into a semi-circle within seconds and your eyes can no longer stand to look straight at the miracle.

The pattern of the waves seemed to be in worship. Birds fly by skimming the surface of the waters and I am struck by their inability to worry. It feels as if the whole earth is singing his praises, rejoicing in the sun's obedience to the command of an almighty God.

ARISE!

All that is within me stirs and I know Jesus is sitting with me on the beach and I marvel at how comfortable I feel in his presence. My innermost being has warmth that sneaks up into my heart fanning a burning flame.

My mind races wanting to ask him how to solve this issue, or what to expect in a particular situation. And I feel more heat and a stirring of love in my heart as he says: May I just love you at this moment?

Yes!

It requires my complete surrender, with eyes to see and ears to hear, what the creator of the universe has to say to me. This same God who just woke up the whole world with his rising sun, wants to allow the risen Son to love me.

I lay in the sand and let my heart be overcome by his love for me. As he drenches me in unexpected reminders of love and mercy, my to-do list seems to vanish. Renewed, I commit my day to him. Whatever he wants, he will lead me. My job is to receive his love, hear his voice and ARISE."

REFLECTION

PAUSE:

Spend a few minutes in silence, settling into a comfortable place where you can allow your body to relax. If there are a few areas that you are still tight or tense, notice that and take a couple deep breaths to release the tension and offer it to God.

PONDER:

- After reading the story, what struck you the most?
- Were there some themes you resonated with?
- Themes that you noticed a resistance within you?
- I invite you to read Lamentations 3:22-24 (NIV)

"Because of the Lord's great love, we are not consumed, for his compassion never fails. They are new every morning; great is your faithfulness. I say to myself, "The Lord is my portion; therefore, I will wait for him."

What word or phrase stood out for you?

PRAY:

Talk with God about it; then, ask God what he would like to say to you about it?

PRACTICE:

Together with God, consider one concrete action step you can take today based on what you heard, read, or experienced during this time.

CLOSING PRAYER (OPTIONAL OR YOUR OWN WORDS)

Dear Lord, If I missed an opportunity to praise you or serve you yesterday, please show me. I thank you that your mercies are new every morning and I have a fresh start.
In Jesus Name, Amen!
*Megan Schrieber: Ocean City, NJ

JOURNAL ENTRY

Gardening*

∞

"The kingdom of heaven is like a mustard seed,
which a man took and planted in his field."
Matthew 13:31-32 (NIV)

"Mommy, what does that mean?" I asked. At five years old, I couldn't yet read the words on the framed cross stitch that hung in our dining room.

My mother replied in her musical voice
"Who plants a seed
Beneath the sod
And waits to see
Believes in God."

I've remembered that verse ever since, but I didn't grasp its miraculous meaning until recently.

As a little girl, I got dirty often. Even outdoors, bare feet pleased me more than the prettiest of shoes. Mud pies, leaf soup, bird feathers, and smooth pebbles were among my chief treasures.

Perhaps in an effort to redirect my errant earthy endeavors, mom gave me a small flower bed of my own to plant however I saw fit. It was only about two feet by four feet, but I was only six years old. It was perfect. I filled it with colorful zinnias that we sowed from seed in egg cartons, snapdragon plugs, and in later years with petunias in my favorite salmon pink hue.

In the thick of summer a fat reddish toad would take up residence at the base of the lamppost which marked one corner of my garden. I liked to visit and watch him feasting on the insects that teemed through the fragrant night air.

My affinity for dirt did not dissipate in adolescence, as many would expect and as my mother might secretly have hoped. My interests shifted to horses and I spent long hours grooming them or riding bareback through woods and over fields, and generally accumulating plenty of grass stains and dust that mingled with the horse sweat. On the bright side, I learned to wash my own laundry at a fairly early age.

Eventually though, so-called "real life" took priority. I became a serious student, went away to college in a big city, and started a career as an ambitious, mobile young professional. My life became practically cosmopolitan. Horses receded into memory, and flowers faded from importance.

Fast forward to spring of 2020. What a time to be alive! In mid-March, quarantine due to the corona pandemic cancelled all events I had planned, and my newest career in real estate was effectively brought to a complete halt by the governor's executive order.

I lived with my sister, who is also a realtor, in a small house with a backyard. I remember the night when everything seemed to be shutting down or falling apart, and it looked like the world was ending. Even if we could stay safe and healthy, and even if we never ran out of toilet paper or wine, we had nothing to do, no idea how we would make any money, pay the bills, or put food on the table. We had no control. I remember a desperate rosary, uncommon tears, and a wordless hug.

"Somehow," I said, "We will get through. I don't know how. But we will."

The next morning, I went rummaging in my basement to pull out fistfuls of tattered, half-empty old seed packets, and little jars holding more seeds from grocery store produce, or attractive flowers I had found growing in the parking lot borders the previous autumn.

With the income freeze, I implemented a near-freeze on spending too. "Reuse" was the mantra of the garden, and free materials made up the bulk of my growing medium. I asked family and friends for whatever precious waste I could cart away. Our garden soil was enriched by kitchen compost, decaying leaves, potash, the dark loose soil that accumulates under heaps of dead brush, old straw that had served as bedding for chickens, and horse manure.

I began to sow. I sowed tomatoes, peppers, and butternut squash. I sowed spinach, chard, lettuce, and kale. I sowed marigolds, sweet peas, onions, and carrots. I sowed good ole faithful zinnias, morning glories, hollyhocks, coneflowers, daisies, and sunflowers.

I sowed seeds in cardboard egg cartons, in unused plastic storage bins, in empty plant pots, in one raised garden bed of commercial construction, one I cobbled together out of extra PVC planks, and another one my sister wove cleverly out of supple cherry tree branches. I sowed in the front of my house where the neighbors could see, and much more in the back. I sowed in the soil beneath our windows and beside our doors. I sowed in an old ruined red wheelbarrow I had found discarded on a curb, and in the woven plastic sacks that held livestock feed. I sowed in the narrow strip of terraced bank that borders our driveway, and in pots on the weather beaten back deck.

I planted the seeds, and then I waited to see.

Hope consists of nothing more and nothing less.

For days, nothing happened. My eager eyes met only bare moist soil every morning and every evening as I scrutinized the windowsill nurseries. After a wait long enough to try my stir-crazy patience, but short enough to fill me with wonder, something happened. In the pots holding my squash seeds, a crumb of sod on the surface shifted. Then a thick pale tender shoot peeked out from underneath, with a fat head bowed. The wiry sunflower seedlings stretched resolutely for the light, even while their little guide leaves remained pinched inside the hollow dry seed husks. The years-old tomato seeds exceeded feeble expectations when they erupted in masse with their outspread leaves. They reminded me of a mob dancing at the YMCA, but that's probably just because by mid-April in quarantine, I missed crowds pretty badly.

Outdoors in my garden beds, things were slowed down by an unusually cold spring but still, life stirred there and would not be stopped. There are few sights more precious and miraculous than the infinitesimal early leaves of a lettuce plant. They're so tiny and bright at first appearance they look more like little pinpricks of green light shining magically through the secretive soil.

Besides for keeping me busy, drawing me outdoors, and generally preserving my sanity in dark times, these plants are lifesavers. The garden has fed and blessed us all summer long in fruit and flower, and it's not even finished yet.

Business and society seem to be slowly, haltingly coming back to life. The future is still rife with uncertainty, and almost nothing is within my control. But in this is hope encapsulated:

Who plants a seed
Beneath the sod
And waits to see
Believes in God.

Let us keep planting our seeds, come what may.

REFLECTION

PAUSE:

Spend a few minutes in silence, settling into a comfortable place where you can allow your body to relax. If there are a few areas that you are still tight or tense, notice that and take a couple deep breaths to release the tension and offer it to God.

PONDER:

- After reading the story, what struck you the most?
- Were there some themes you resonated with?
- Themes that you noticed a resistance within you?
- I invite you to read Matthew 13:31-32

He told them another parable: "The kingdom of heaven is like a mustard seed, which man took and planted in his field. Though it is the smallest of all seeds, yet when it grows, it is the largest of garden plants and becomes a tree, so that the birds come and perch in its branches."

What word or phrase stood out for you?

PRAY:

Talk with God about it; then, ask God what he would like to say to you about it?

PRACTICE:

Together with God, consider one concrete action step you can take today based on what you heard, read, or experienced during this time.

CLOSING PRAYER (OPTIONAL OR YOUR OWN):

Dear Lord,
Thank you for sharing with me a small sliver of what it is like to live prosperously in your kingdom. Help me to realize that planting even the smallest of seeds can reap a crop in abundance. When I am among family, friends, and co-workers today, may my words and actions reflect the hope that is only found in you. In Jesus Name, Amen!
*Chiara Cardone: Back yard: Pennsylvania

JOURNAL ENTRY

Contributor's
Listed in Order of Entries

∞

A Pilgrim's Journey: John Chesters
Peak Encounter Ministries Retreat Leader
www.peakencounter.org
Care of Creation: Ricardo Simmonds
Environmental Policy Advisor at United States Conference of
Catholic Bishops
Founder and Former Director, Creatio
www.creatio.org
Appalachian Mountain Road: Jeff Klein
Retreat Leadership Team, Peak Encounter Ministries
www.peakencounter.org
Rustic Cabin: Jen Messing, MTS
www.idretreats.org
Dark Stroll: Sean Cavanaugh
sculptedinchrist@gmail.com
Walk Through the Season: Bill Donaghy, M.A.
Faculty Member/Speaker/Lecturer/Curriculum Specialist
Theology of the Body Institute – "The Way of Beauty" Course
www.TOBinstitute.org
Bus to Umbria: Kelly Wahlquist
Founder, WINE (Women in the New Evangelization)
Director, Archbishop Harry J Flynn Catechetical Institute
www.catholicvinyard.com

Scuba Diving: Elizabeth Hoisington
Joyful mother
Star Gazing: Mickey Fairorth
Seminarian, Saint Charles Seminary
Hot Air Balloon: Heather Makowicz
Certified Spiritual Director and Counselor
www.peakencounter.org/heathermakowicz.com
Backpacking: Trix
Canyoneering: Heather Makowicz
Certified Spiritual Director and Counselor
www.peakencounter.org/heathermakowicz.com
Rock Climbing: Chiara Cardone
Nativity BVM Parish in Media, PA.
cabbagesandkings.com blog
Mountain Climbing: James Delany
Former Board Member, Catholic Leadership Institute
Whitewater Rafting: Christin Zimmer
www.czimmer.com
Surfing: Bear and Jeremiah Woznick
Executive Producer/The Bear Woznick Adventure Radio Show
www.DeepAdventure.com
Sailing: Sarah Christmyer
Adjunct Faculty Member, Saint Charles Borromeo Seminary
www.comeintotheword.com
Caving: Tom Zimmer
Executive Director, COR Expeditions
www.Corexpeditions.org
Ice Climbing: Father Nathan Cromly
CSJ; President, The Saint John Institute
www.saintjohninstitute.org
Desert Trek: Heather Makowicz
Peak Encounter Ministries Founder, Certified Spiritual
Director, Counselor
www.peakencounter.org / heathermakowicz.com
Paddle Boarding: Heather Makowicz
Peak Encounter Ministries Founder, Certified Spiritual
Director, Counselor

www.peakencounter.org / heathermakowicz.com
Stemming: Heather Makowicz
Peak Encounter Ministries Founder, Certified Spiritual Director and Counselor
www.peakencounter.org / heathermakowicz.com
Fishing: Lori Blake-Tedjeske
Peak Encounter Ministries, Strategic Leadership Team Leader
www.peakencouter.org
Photography: Brett Illig
www.journeyofasoul.me blog
Watching Birds: Father Henry M. Jordanek,O. Praem
www.daylesford.org
Sunset: Jeannine Peters
Certified Spiritual Director
www.jeanninepeters.com
Waterfall Plunge: Heather Makowicz
Peak Encounter Ministries Founder, Certified Spiritual Director, Counselor
www.peakencounter.org / heathermakowicz.com
The Desert: Heather Makowicz
Peak Encounter Ministries Founder, Certified Spiritual Director, Counselor
www.peakencounter.org / heathermakowicz.com
The Bench: Elizabeth Hoisington
Joyful Mother
Sunrise: Megan Schreiber
Founder and Principal Consultant; Harvest Consulting
www.harvest.consulting
Gardening: Chiara Cardone
Nativity BVM Parish in Media, PA.
cabbagesandkings.com blog

Works Cited

Benedict XVI (Joseph Ratzinger), *Principles of Catholic Theology: Building Stones for a Fundamental Theology*. Ignatius Press, 1987.

Benedict XVI. "Shockingly Beautiful." *The Art Of Vision*, 4 Sept. 2015, www.theartofvision.com/2012/12/26/shockingly-beautiful/.

"Blessed Cardinal John Henry Newman." *Faith Magazine*, Diocese of Lansing, 10 Sept. 2019, faithmag.com/blessed-cardinal-john-henry-newman.

Ciszek, Walter J., and Daniel L. Flaherty. *With God in Russia*. Ignatius Press, 1997.

Denver, John. "Annie's Song." *Back Home Again*, Milt Okun, RCA Records.

Francis. *Laudato Si'*. 24 May 2015, www.vatican.va/content/francesco/en/encyclicals/documents/papa-francesco_20150524_enciclica-laudato-si.html.

Houselander, Caryll. *Reed of God*. Ave Maria Press, 2006.

Ivereigh, Austen. *The Great Reformer: Francis and the Making of a Radical Pope*. Picador, 2015.

John Paul II. *Letter to Artists*. 4 Apr. 1999, www.vatican.va/content/john-paul-ii/en/letters/1999/documents/hf_jp-ii_let_23041999_artists.html.

John Paul II. *XXIII World Day for Peace 1990, Peace with God the Creator, Peace with All of Creation.* 1 Jan. 1990, www.vatican.va/content/john-paul-ii/en/messages/peace/documents/hf_jp-ii_mes_19891208_xxiii-world-day-for-peace.html.

Lewis, C. S. *Miracles.* Macmillian, 1978.

"Online Conversation: Habits, Home & the Human Heart, with James K.A. Smith." *The Trinity Forum*, www.ttf.org/portfolios/online-conversation-james-k-a-smith/.

Rilke, Rainer Maria. "Go to the Limits of Your Longing." Translated by Joanna Macy, *The On Being Project*, 9 Oct. 2020, onbeing.org/poetry/go-to-the-limits-of-your-longing/.

Shakespeare, William. *As You Like It. The Folger Shakespeare*, 25 June 2020, shakespeare.folger.edu/shakespeares-works/as-you-like-it/.

Sheen, Fulton J., and Yousuf Karsh. *These Are the Sacraments.* Hawthorn Books, Inc., 1962.

CPSIA information can be obtained
at www.ICGtesting.com
Printed in the USA
BVHW090644060521
606603BV00003B/3